A COLLECTION OF SONGS, POEMS & AMUSING STORIES

Nuala Harnett

First published in Ireland in 2006 by

H & R PUBLISHING

2(b) Ormond Lane, Ormond Road, Drumcondra, Dublin 9

A CIP catalogue record for this book is available from the National Library of Ireland and the British Library.

Photography by Pat Rooney

ISBN: 0-9537609-1-X

Designed and Produced by Rooney Media Graphics Limited 2(b) Ormond Lane, Ormond Road, Drumcondra, Dublin 9
Telephone: + 353 1 797 8774 Facsimile: + 353 1 797 8777 Email: rooneygx@iol.ie Website: www.rooneymedia.com

Printed by Future Print

To obtain a copy of the first book of Party Pieces, Email: rooneygx@iol.ie

Introduction

The Irish really know how to have a good party. They don't sit back and wait to be entertained, but join in and enter into the spirit of the occasion. Consequently, a great atmosphere of warmth and camaraderie is created.

Most Irish parties develop into a "sing-song" where someone stands up and sings a song, someone else follows, and often recitations and stories are told.

This book is for you to have your own party piece. My first publication, ***"The only book of Party Pieces"****, gave you a useful selection and now, with* ***Party Pieces 2,*** *you have more options.*

In the ***Songs*** *section there are some from musicals, the best "singable" popular songs from over the years, and traditional* ***Irish songs*** *and ballads.*

The ***Poems*** *are varied. Most are light-hearted and fun, and some are more thoughtful and sentimental.*

I hope the ***Amusing Stories*** *will make you smile and that you will enjoy telling them.*

It is a good idea to learn off your party piece and perhaps practise it at home before you have "to do your turn." However, if you feel words will fail you, bring the book.

Have a great time and enter into the party spirit!

Nuala Harnett

Nuala Harnett

Contents

Songs

Poems

Amusing Stories

Songs

Here you will find a wide selection of songs. Some are from well-known musicals, and others are popular songs which have become classics. You also have a number of the most beautiful Irish ballads.

If you are a reasonable singer and can hold a tune, pick a song with lots of melody. Learn the words well and, when performing it, hold your head up and sing out.

If you have an average voice, choose a catchy song with a good beat and not too wide a range. Smile at your audience and encourage them to join in the chorus.

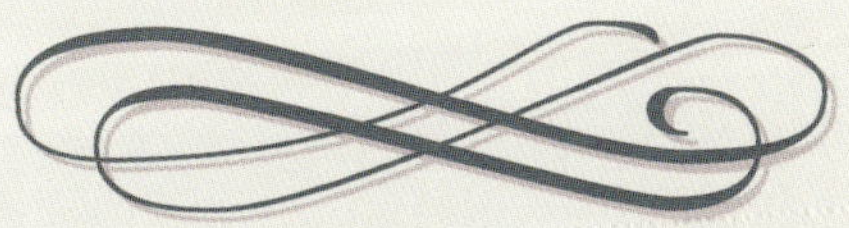

Super Trouper

Andersson/Ulvaeus

Super Trouper beams are gonna blind me
But I won't feel blue, like I always do
'Cause somewhere in the crowd there's you

I was sick and tired of everything
When I called you last night from Glasgow
All I do is eat and sleep and sing
Wishing every show was the last show
So imagine I was glad to hear you're coming
Suddenly I feel all right
And it's gonna be so different
When I'm on the stage tonight

Refrain
Tonight the
Super Trouper lights are gonna find me
Shining like the sun, smiling having fun
Feeling like a number one
Tonight the
Super Trouper beams are gonna blind me
But I won't feel blue, like I always do
'Cause somewhere in the crowd there's you

Facing twenty thousand of your friends
How can anyone be so lonely
Part of a success that never ends
Still I'm thinking about you only
There are moments when
I think I'm going crazy
But it's gonna be alright
Everything will be so different
When I'm on the stage tonight

Refrain Tonight the.....

So I'll be there when you arrive
The sight of you will prove
To me I'm still alive
And when you take me in your arms
And hold me tight
I know it's gonna mean so much tonight

Refrain Tonight the......

Climb Ev'ry Mountain

Hammerstein/Rodgers

Climb ev'ry mountain, search high and low
Follow ev'ry by-way, every path you know
Climb ev'ry mountain, ford ev'ry stream
Follow ev'ry rainbow, 'till you find your dream

A dream that will need all the love you can give
Everyday of your life for as long as you live
Climb ev'ry mountain, ford ev'ry stream
Follow ev'ry rainbow 'till you find your dream

Repeat A dream that.......

What a Wonderful World

Weiss/Thiele

I see trees of green, red roses too
I see them bloom for me and you
And I think to myself:
"What a wonderful world!"

I see skies of blue and clouds of white
The bright blessed day, the dark sacred night
And I think to myself:
"What a wonderful world!"

The colors of the rainbow so pretty in the sky
Are also on the faces of people going by
I see friends shaking hands saying
"How do you do."
They're really saying: "I love you!"

I hear babies crying I watch them grow
They'll learn much more than I'll ever know
And I think to myself:
"What a wonderful world!"
Yes, I think to myself:
"What a wonderful world!"

Take Me Home, Country Roads

Danoff/Nivert/Denver

Almost heaven, West Virgina
Blue Ridge Mountains,
Shenandoah River
Life is old there, older than the trees
Younger than the mountains,
Flowing like the breeze.

Refrain
Country roads, take me home
To the place I belong
West Virginia, mountain mama
Take me home, country roads.

All my memories gather 'round her
Miner's lady, stranger to blue water
Dark and dusky, painted on the sky
Misty taste of moonshine, teardrop in my eye.

Refrain Country roads.....

I hear her voice, in the morning hour she calls me
Radio reminds me of my home far away
Driving down the road I get a feeling
That I should have been home yesterday, yesterday

Refrain Country roads.....

The Black Velvet Band

As I was walking down Broadway,
Not intending to stay very long
I met with a frolicsome damsel
As she came tripping along.
A gold watch she took out of her pocket
And placed it right into my hand
On the very first time that I saw her;
Bad luck to the black velvet band

Refrain
Her eyes they shone like diamonds;
You'd think she was queen of the land
With her hair thrown over her shoulder;
Tied up with a black velvet band.

'Twas in the town of Kilkenny;
An apprentice to trade I was bound
With gaiety and bright amusement
To see all the days go around
Till misfortune and trouble came over me
Which forced me to stray from the land
Far away from my friends and relations;
Betrayed by the black velvet band.

Refrain Her eyes they shone......

Before judge and jury next morning
The both of us did appear
A gentleman swore to his jewellery
And the case against us was clear
Seven long years' transportation
Away down to Van Diemen's Land

Far away from my friends and relations
To follow the black velvet band.

Refrain Her eyes they shone......

Now all you brave young Irish lads,
A warning please gather from me
Beware of the pretty young damsels
You meet all around Kilkenny
They'll treat you with whiskey and porter
Until you're unable to stand
And before you have time for to leave them
You'll be sent down to Van Diemen's Land.

Refrain Her eyes they shone......

Always On My Mind

Thompson, James and Christopher

Maybe I didn't treat you
Quite as good as I should have
Maybe I didn't love you
Quite as often as I could have
Little things I should have said and done
I just never took the time

You were always on my mind
You were always on my mind

Tell me, tell me that your
Sweet love hasn't died
Give me, give me one more chance
To keep you satisfied, satisfied

Maybe I didn't hold you
All those lonely, lonely times
And I guess I never told you
I'm so happy that you're mine
If I make you feel second best
Girl, I'm sorry I was blind

You were always on my mind
You were always on my mind

Daydream Believer

John Stewart

Oh, I could hide 'neath the wings
Of the bluebird as she sings.
The six o'clock alarm would never ring.
Whoops it's ringing and I rise,
Wipe the sleep out of my eyes.
My shavin' razor's cold and it stings.

Refrain
Cheer up, sleepy Jean.
Oh, what can it mean.
To a daydream believer
And a homecoming
queen.

You once thought of me
As a white knight on a
steed.
Now you know how
happy I can be.
Oh, and our good times
start and end
Without dollar one to spend.
But how much, baby, do we really need.

Refrain (twice) Cheer up, sleepy Jean.......

TREK
TREK

Dancing Queen

Andersson/Ulvaeus

You can dance, you can jive
Having the time of your life
See that girl, watch that scene
Dig in the Dancing Queen

Friday night and the lights are low
Looking out for the place to go
Where they play the right music
Getting in the swing
You come in to look for a king
Anybody could be that guy
Night is young and the music's high
With a bit of rock music
Everything is fine
You're in the mood for a dance
And when you get the chance...

Refrain
You are the Dancing Queen
Young and sweet, only seventeen
Dancing Queen feel the beat
From the tambourine
You can dance, you can jive
Having the time of your life
See that girl, watch that scene
Dig in the Dancing Queen

You're a teaser, you turn 'em on
Leave them burning and then you're gone
Looking out for another, anyone will do
You're in the mood for a dance
And when you get the chance...

Refrain You are the......

Are You Lonesome Tonight?

Roy Turk and Lou Handman

Are you lonesome tonight?
Do you miss me tonight?
Are you sorry we drifted apart?
Does your memory stray
To a bright sunny day
When I kissed you
And called you sweetheart?

Do the chairs in your parlor
Seem empty and bare?
Do you gaze at your doorstep
And picture me there?
Is your heart filled with pain
Shall I come back again?
Tell me dear
Are you lonesome tonight?

Close to You

Hal David/Burt Bacharach

Why do birds suddenly appear
Every time you are near?
Just like me, they long to be
Close to you.

Why do stars fall down from the sky
Every time you walk by?
Just like me, they long to be
Close to you.

On the day that you were born
The angels got together
And decided to create a dream come true
So they sprinkled moon dust in your hair
Of gold and starlight in your eyes of blue.

That is why all the girls in town
Follow you all around.
Just like me, they long to be
Close to you.

Just like me, they long to be
Close to you.

My Heart Will Go On

James Horner/Will Jennings

Every night in my dreams
I see you, I feel you.
That is how I know you go on.
Far across the distance
And spaces between us
You have come to show you go on.

Refrain
Near, far, wherever you are
I believe that the heart does go on
Once more you open the door
And you're here in my heart
And my heart will go on and on

Love can touch us one time
And last for a lifetime
And never let go till we're gone
Love was when I loved you
One true time I hold to
In my life we'll always go on

Refrain Near, far......

You're here, there's nothing I fear,
And I know that my heart will go on
We'll stay forever this way
You are safe in my heart
And my heart will go on and on

The Winner Takes It All

Andersson/Ulvaeus

I don't wanna talk about the things
We've gone through
Though it's hurting me, now it's history
I've played all my cards
And that's what you've done too
Nothing more to say, no more ace to play

The winner takes it all, the loser standing small
Beside the victory, that's her destiny

I was in your arms, thinking I belonged there
I figured it made sense, building me a fence
Building me a home, thinking I'd be strong there
But I was a fool, playing by the rules

The gods may throw a dice,
Their minds as cold as ice
And someone way down here,
Loses someone dear
The winner takes it all, the loser has to fall
It's simple and it's plain, why should I complain

But tell me does she kiss, like I used to kiss you?
Does it feel the same, when she calls your name?
Somewhere deep inside
You must know I miss you
But what can I say, rules must be obeyed

The judges will decide, the likes of me abide
Spectators of the show, always staying low
The game is on again, a lover or a friend
A big thing or a small, the winner takes it all

I don't wanna talk if it makes you feel sad
And I understand,
You've come to shake my hand
I apologize if it makes you feel bad
Seeing me so tense, no self-confidence
But you see

The winner takes it all
The winner takes it all .....

Dicey Reilly

Refrain
Poor aul Dicey Riley she has taken to the sup.
Poor aul Dicey Riley she will never give it up.
For it's off each mornin' to the hock
Where she goes in for another little drop.
Ah the heart of the rowl is Dicey Riley.

She walks along Fitzgibbon Street
With an independent air
And then it's down by Summerhill
Where the people stop and stare
She says "It's nearly half past one,
It's time I had another little one"
Ah the heart of the rowl is Dicey Reilly.

Refrain Poor aul Dicey Riley......

She owns a little sweet shop
At the corner of the street
And every evening after school
I go to wash her feet
She leaves me there to mind the shop
While she nips in for another little drop
Ah the heart of the rowl is Dicey Reilly.

Refrain Poor aul Dicey Riley......

Ring of Fire

Merle Kilgore/June Carter

Love is a burning thing
And it makes a fiery ring
Bound by wild desire
I fell into a ring of fire

Refrain
I fell into a burning ring of fire
I went down, down, down
And the flames went higher
And it burns, burns, burns
The ring of fire, the ring of fire

The taste of love is sweet
When hearts like ours meet
I fell for you like a child
Oh, but the fire went wild

Refrain I fell into........

Everything I Do, I Do It For You

Adams/Lange/Kamen

Look into my eyes - you will see
What you mean to me
Search your heart - search your soul
And when you find me there
You'll search no more
Don't tell me it's not worth tryin' for
You can't tell me it's not worth dyin' for
You know it's true
Everything I do - I do it for you

Look into my heart - you will find
There's nothin' there to hide
Take me as I am - take my life
I would give it all - I would sacrifice
Don't tell me it's not worth fightin' for
I can't help it - there's nothin' I want more
Ya know it's true
Everything I do - I do it for you

There's no love - like your love
And no other - could give more love
There's nowhere - unless you're there
All the time - all the way

Don't tell me it's not worth tryin' for
I can't help it - there's nothin' I want more
I would fight for you - I'd lie for you
Walk the wire for you - ya, I'd die for you
You know it's true
Everything I do - I do it for you

For Once In My Life

Ronald Miller/Orlando Murden

For once in my life I have
Someone who needs me
Someone I've needed so long
For once, unafraid,
I can go where life leads me
Somehow I know I'll be strong
For once I can touch
What my heart used to dream of
Long before I knew
Oooh someone warm like you
Would make my dream come true

For once in my life
I won't let sorrow hurt me
Not like it hurt me before
For once I have someone
I know won't desert me
I'm not alone anymore
For once, I can say,
This is mine,
you can't take it
As long as I know
I have love,
I can make it
For once in my life,
I have someone
who needs me

Repeat second Verse

The Spanish Lady

As I rode down through Dublin city at the hour of twelve at night,
Who should I see but a Spanish lady washing her feet by candle light.
First she washed them then she dried them over a fire of amber coal.
In all my life I ne'er did see a-a maid so sweet about the soul.

Refrain
Whack fol the toor-a-loor-a la-ad-ie, whack fol the toor-a-loor-a lay.
Whack fol the toor-a-loor-a la-ad-ie, whack fol the toor-a-loor-a lay.

As I came back through Dublin city at the hour of half past eight

Who should I spy but the Spanish Lady brushing her hair in the broad daylight
First she tossed it then she brushed it; on her lap was a silver comb
In all my life I ne'er did see a maid so fair since I did roam.

Refrain Whack fol the.........

Catch a Falling Star

Lee Pockriss/Paul Vance

Catch a falling star and put it in your pocket
Never let it fade away
Catch a falling star and put it in your pocket
Save it for a rainy day

For love may come and tap you on the shoulder
Some starless night
Just in case you feel you want to hold her
You'll have a pocketful of starlight

Catch a falling star and put it in your pocket
Never let it fade away
Catch a falling star and put it in your pocket
Save it for a rainy day
For when your troubles start multiplyin'
And they just might
It's easy to forget them without tryin'
With just a pocketful of starlight

Catch a falling star and put it in your pocket
Never let it fade away
Catch a falling star and put it in your pocket
Save it for a rainy day

Don't Cry For Me, Argentina

Webber/Rice

It won't be easy, you'll think it strange
When I try to explain how I feel
That I still need your love after all that I've done
You won't believe me
All you will see is a girl you once knew
Although she's dressed up to the nines
At sixes and sevens with you

I had to let it happen; I had to change
Couldn't stay all my life down at heel
Looking out of the window
Staying out of the sun
So I chose freedom
Running around trying everything new
But nothing impressed me at all
I never expected it to

Refrain
Don't cry for me, Argentina
The truth is I never left you
All through my wild days
My mad existence I kept my promise
Don't keep your distance

And as for fortune, and as for fame
I never invited them in
Though it seemed to the world
They were all I desired
They are illusions
They're not the solutions
They promised to be
The answer was here all the time
I love you and hope you love me

Refrain Don't cry for me.....

Have I said too much?
There's nothing more
I can think of to say to you
But all you have to do is look at me
To know that every word is true.

The Dublin Saunter

I've been north and I've been south
And I've been east and west,
I've been just a rolling stone.
Yet there's one place on this earth
I've always liked the best
Just a little town I call my own.

Refrain
Dublin can be heaven with coffee at eleven,
And a stroll in Stephen's Green;
There's no need to hurry,
There's no need to worry:
You're a king and the lady's a queen.
Grafton Street's a wonderland,
There's magic in the air;
There are diamonds in the lady's eyes
And gold dust in her hair;
And if you don't believe me,
Come and meet me there,
In Dublin on a sunny summer morning.

I've been here and I've been there,
I've sought the rainbow's end;
But no crock of gold I've found.
Now I know that come what will,
Whatever fate may send,
Here my roots are deep in friendly ground.

Refrain Dublin can be heaven......

LE CLIPPER
CN 208 251

Do You Know Where You're Going to?

Gerry Goffin/Mike Masser

Refrain
Do you know where you're going to?
Do you like the things that life is showing you
Where are you going to, do you know...?

Do you get what you're hoping for
When you look behind you there's no open door
What are you hoping for, do you know...?

Once we were standing still in time
Chasing the fantasies that filled our minds
You knew how I loved you
But my spirit was free
Laughin' at the questions
That you once asked of me

Refrain Do you know........

Now looking back at all we planned
We let so many dreams
Just slip through our hands
Why must we wait so long before we see
How sad the answers to those questions can be

Refrain Do you know........

Nights In White Satin

Justin Hayward

Nights in white satin
Never reaching the end
Letters I've written
Never meaning to send

Beauty I'd always missed
With these eyes before
Just what the truth is
I can't say any more

'Cause I love you, yes I love you
Oh how I love you

Gazing at people
Some hand in hand
Just what I'm going through
They can't understand

Some try to tell me
Thoughts they cannot defend
Just what you want to be
You'll be in the end

And I love you, yes I love you
Oh how I love you, oh

Fields Of Gold

Sting

You'll remember me when the west wind moves
Upon the fields of barley
You'll forget the sun in his jealous sky
As we walk in the fields of gold

So she took her love for to gaze a while
Upon the fields of barley
In his arms she fell as her hair came down
Among the fields of gold

Will you stay with me, will you be my love
Among the fields of barley
We'll forget the sun in his jealous sky
As we lie in the fields of gold

See the west wind move like a lover so
Upon the fields of barley
Feel her body rise when you kiss her mouth
Among the fields of gold

I never made promises lightly
And there have been some that I've broken
But I swear in the days still left
We'll walk in the fields of gold
We'll walk in the fields of gold

Many years have passed since those summer days
Among the fields of barley
See the children run as the sun goes down
Among the fields of gold
You'll remember me when the west wind moves
Upon the fields of barley
You can tell the sun in his jealous sky
When we walked in the fields of gold
When we walked in the fields of gold

These Boots Are Made For Walkin'

Lee Hazelwood

You keep sayin' you've got somethin' for me,
Somethin' you call love, but confess
You've been a-messin',
Where you shouldna' been a-messin',
And now someone else is getting all your best.

Refrain
These boots are made for walkin',
And that's just what they'll do
One of these days these boots are gonna'
Walk all over you.

You keep lyin' when you oughta' be truth-in',
You keep losin' when you oughta' not bet
You keep same-in' when you oughta' be changin',
And now right is right, and you ain't been right yet.

Refrain These boots are.......

You keep playin' where you shouldn't be playin'
You keep thinkin' that you'll never get burnt.
I just found me a brand new box of matches,
And what he knows you ain't got time to learn.

Refrain These boots are.......

It's Not Unusual

Mills/Reed

It's not unusual to be loved by anyone
It's not unusual to have fun with anyone
But when I see you hanging about with anyone
It's not unusual to see me cry, oh I wanna' die

It's not unusual to go out at any time
But when I see you out and about
It's such a crime
If you should ever want to be loved by anyone,
It's not unusual
It happens every day no matter what you say
You find it happens all the time
Love will never do what you want it to
Why can't this crazy love be mine

It's not unusual to be mad with anyone
It's not unusual to be sad with anyone
But if I ever find that you've changed at anytime
It's not unusual to find that I'm in love with you
Whoa-oh-oh-oh-oh

The Rose of Tralee

The pale moon was rising above the green mountain,
The sun was declining beneath the blue sea,
When I strayed with my love to the pure crystal fountain
That stands in the beautiful vale of Tralee

She was lovely and fair as the rose of the summer,
Yet 'twas not her beauty alone that won me,
Oh no, 'twas the truth in her eyes ever dawning
That made me love Mary, the Rose of Tralee

The cool shades of evening their mantle were spreading,
And Mary, all smiling, was listening to me,
The moon through the valley her pale rays was shedding
When I won the heart of the Rose of Tralee

Tho' lovely and fair as the rose of the summer,
Yet 'twas not her beauty alone that won me,
Oh no, 'twas the truth in her eyes ever dawning
That made me love Mary, the Rose of Tralee

Leavin' On a Jet Plane

John Denver

All my bags are packed, I'm ready to go
I'm standin' here, outside your door
I hate to wake you up to say good-bye.
But the dawn is breakin', it's early morn
Taxi's waitin', he's blowin' his horn
Already I'm so lonesome I could cry.

Refrain
So kiss me and smile for me
Tell me that you'll wait for me
Hold me like you'll never let me go.
I'm leavin' on a jet plane
Don't know when I'll be back again
Oh, babe, I hate to go.

There's so many times I've let you down
So many times I've played around
I tell you now, they don't mean a thing.
Every place I go I think of you
Every song I sing, I sing for you.
When I come back, I'll wear your wedding ring.

Refrain So kiss me.....

Now the time has come to leave you
One more time, let me kiss you.
Then close your eyes, I'll be on my way.
Dream about the days to come
When I won't have to leave alone
About the time I won't have to say

Refrain So kiss me.....

He Ain't Heavy, He's My Brother

Bobby Scott and Bob Russell

The road is long
With many a winding turn
That leads us to who knows where
Who knows when, but I'm strong
Strong enough to carry him
He ain't heavy, he's my brother

So on we go
His welfare is of my concern
No burden is he to bear
We'll get there, for I know
He would not encumber me
He ain't heavy, he's my brother

If I'm laden at all
I'm laden with sadness
That everyone's heart
Isn't filled with the gladness
Of love for one another

It's a long, long road
From which there is no return
While we're on the way to there
Why not share, and the load
Doesn't weigh me down at all
He ain't heavy, he's my brother

I Believe

Drake/Graham/Shirl/Stillman

I believe for every drop of rain that falls
A flower grows
I believe that somewhere in the darkest night
A candle glows
I believe for everyone who goes astray
Someone will come to show the way
I believe, I believe

I believe above the storm the smallest prayer
Will still be heard
I believe that someone in the great somewhere
Hears every word
Every time I hear a newborn baby cry
Or touch a leaf or see the sky
Then I know why, I believe

Every time I hear a newborn baby cry
Or touch a leaf or see the sky
Then I know why I believe.

Magic, Moments,

David/Bacharach

Magic Moments when two hearts are carin'
Magic moments, memories we've been sharin'
I'll never forget the moment we kissed,
The night of the hayride,
The way that we hugged to try to keep warm,
While takin' a sleigh ride.

Refrain
Magic moments, memories we've been sharin'
Magic moments, when two hearts are carin'
Time can't erase the memory of
These magic moments filled with love!

The telephone call that tied up the line,
For hours and hours,
The Saturday dance, I got up the nerve,
To send you some flowers.

Refrain Magic, moments........

The way that we cheered whenever our team
Was scoring a touchdown!
The time that the floor fell out of my car,
When I put the clutch down!
The penny arcade, the games that we played,
The fun and the prizes!
The Halloween hop, when everyone came
In funny disguises.
Magic moments filled with love!

Delilah

Tom Jones

I saw the light on the night
That I passed by her window
I saw the flickering shadows
Of love on her blind
She was my woman
As she deceived me I watched
And went out of my mind

My, my, my, Delilah, why, why, why, Delilah
I could see that girl was no good for me
But I was lost like a slave that no man could free

At break of day when that man drove away,
I was waiting
I crossed the street to her house
And she opened the door
She stood there laughing
I felt the knife in my hand
And she laughed no more

My, my, my Delilah, why, why, why Delilah
So before they come to break down the door
Forgive me Delilah I just couldn't take any more

My, my, my Delilah, why, why, why Delilah
So before they come to break down the door
Forgive me Delilah I just couldn't take any more
Forgive me Delilah I just couldn't take any more

Money Money Money

Andersson/Ulvaeus

I work all night, I work all day
To pay the bills I have to pay, ain't it sad
And still there never seems to be
A single penny left for me,that's too bad
In my dreams I have a plan
If I got me a wealthy man
I wouldn't have to work at all
I'd fool around and have a ball...

Refrain
Money, money, money, must be funny
In the rich man's world
Money, money, money, always sunny
In the rich man's world, aha-ahaaa
All the things I could do
If I had a little money
It's a rich man's world

A man like that is hard to find but
I can't get him off my mind, ain't it sad
And if he happens to be free
I bet he wouldn't fancy me, that's too bad
So I must leave, I'll have to go
To Las Vegas or Monaco
And win a fortune in a game
My life will never be the same...

Refrain (twice) Money, money, money......

She Moved Through The Fair

My young love said to me, "My mother won't mind
And my father won't slight you for your lack of kind"
And she stepped away from me and this she did say,
"Oh it will not be long love, till our wedding day".

She went away from me and she moved through the fair
And fondly I watched her move here and move there
And she made her way homeward with one star awake
As the swan in the evening moves over the lake.

Last night 1 did dream that my love she came in
And so softly she came that her feet made no din
And she laid her hand on me and smiling did say
"It will not be long love, till our wedding day"

Bridge Over Troubled Water

Paul Simon

When you're weary, feeling small
When tears are in your eyes
I will dry them all, I'm on your side
When times get rough
And friends just can't be found

Like a bridge over troubled water
I will lay me down
Like a bridge over troubled water
I will lay me down

When you're down and out
When you're on the street
When evening falls so hard
I will comfort you, I'll take your part
When darkness comes
And pain is all around

* Like a bridge over troubled water
I will ease your mind
Like a bridge over troubled water
I will ease your mind

Sail on silver girl, sail on by
Your time has come to shine
All your dreams are on their way
See how they shine
If you need a friend
I'm sailing right behind
Repeat * Like a bridge....

Everytime We Say Goodbye

Cole Porter

Ev'ry time we say goodbye
I die a little
Ev'ry time we say goodbye
I wonder why a little
Why the gods above me
Who must be in the know
Think so little of me
They allow you to go

When you're near there's such an air
Of spring about it,
I can hear a lark somewhere
Begin to sing about it,
There's no love song finer
But how strange the change
From major to minor
Ev'ry time we say goodbye

(Repeat) When you're near ....

On the Street Where You Live

Lerner and Loewe

I have often walked down this street before
But the pavement always stayed
Beneath my feet before
All at once am I several stories high
Knowing I'm on the street where you live

Are there lilac trees in the heart of town?
Can you hear a lark in any other part of town?
Does enchantment pour out of every door?
No, it's just on the street where you live

And oh, the towering feeling
Just to know somehow you are near
The overpowering feeling
That any second you may suddenly appear

People stop and stare, they don't bother me
For there's nowhere else
On earth that I would rather be
Let the time go by, I won't care if I
Can be here on the street where you live

Another Day in Paradise

Phil Collins

She calls out to the man on the street
"Sir, can you help me?
It's cold and I've nowhere to sleep,
Is there somewhere you can tell me?"
He walks on, doesn't look back
He pretends he can't hear her
Starts to whistle as he crosses the street
Seems embarrassed to be there

Refrain
Oh think twice, it's another day for
You and me in paradise
Oh think twice, it's just another day for you,
You and me in paradise, think about it

She calls out to the man on the street
He can see she's been crying
She's got blisters on the soles of her feet
Can't walk but she's trying

Refrain Oh think twice........

Oh lord, is there nothing more anybody can do?
Oh lord, there must be something you can say

You can tell from the lines on her face
You can see that she's been there
Probably been moved on from every place
'Cause she didn't fit in there

Refrain Oh think twice.........

Moon River

Johnny Mercer/Henry Mancini

Moon river wider than a mile
I'm crossing you in style, some day...
Old dream maker, you heart breaker
Wherever you're going, I'm going your way...

Two drifters, off to see the world
There's such a lot of world to see...
We're after the same rainbow's end
Waiting 'round the bend
My Huckleberry friend
Moon River and me..

I'll Tell My Ma

I'll tell my Ma when I go home
The boys won't leave the girls alone.
They pull my hair, they stole my comb
But that's alright till I go home.
She is handsome, she is pretty,
She is the belle of Belfast city.
She is courting one, two , three,
Please won't you tell me who is she.

Albert Mooney says he loves her;
All the boys are fighting for her
They rap at the door and they ring at the bell
Saying "Oh, my true love are you well"
Out she comes as white as snow;
Rings on her fingers, bells on her toes
Jenny Murray says she'll die
If she doesn't get the fella with the roving eye.

Let the wind and the rain and the hail blow high
And the snow come tumbling from the sky
She's as nice as apple pie
And she'll get her own lad by and by,
When she gets a lad of her own
She won't tell her Ma when she goes home
But let them all come as they will;
It's Albert Mooney she loves still.

(Repeat first verse) I'll tell my Ma......

Love Me Tender

Elvis Presley/Vera Matson

Love me tender, love me sweet,
Never let me go.
You have made my life complete,
And I love you so.

Refrain
Love me tender, love me true,
All my dreams fulfill.
For my darlin' I love you,
And I always will.

Love me tender, love me long,
Take me to your heart.
For it's there that I belong,
And we'll never part.

Refrain Love me tender.......

Love me tender, love me dear,
Tell me you are mine.
I'll be yours through all the years,
Till the end of time.

Refrain Love me tender.......

Dream a Little Dream

Gus Kahn/Schwandt/Andree

Stars shining bright above you.
Night breezes seem to whisper, "I love you,"
Birds singing in the sycamore tree.
"Dream a little dream of me."

Say "nighty-night" and kiss me.
Just hold me tight and tell me you'll miss me.
While I'm alone and blue as can be,
Dream a little dream of me.

Stars fading, but I linger on, dear,
Still craving your kiss.
I'm longing to linger 'till dawn, dear,
Just saying this:

Sweet dreams 'till sunbeams find you,
Sweet dreams that leave all worries behind you.
But in your dreams, whatever they be.
Dream a little dream of me.

Fly me to the moon

Bart Howard

Fly me to the Moon
And let me play among the stars
Let me see what spring is like
On Jupiter and Mars
In other words, hold my hand
In other words, darling kiss me

Fill my life with song
And let me sing for ever more
You are all I hope for
All I worship and adore
In other words, please be true
In other words, I love you

Repeat both Verses

Everybody's Talkin'

Fred Neil

Everybody's talkin' at me
I don't hear a word they're sayin'
Only the echoes of my mind
People stop and stare
I can't see their faces
Only the shadows of their eyes

I'm goin' where the sun keeps shinin'
Through the pourin' rain
Goin' where the weather suits my clothes
Bankin' off the northeast winds
Sailin' on a summer breeze
And skippin' over the ocean like a stone

Everybody's talkin' at me
Can't hear a word they're sayin'
Only the echoes of my mind
I won't let you leave my love behind
No I won't let you leave
I won't let you leave my love behind

I Left My Heart In San Francisco

Douglas Cross/George Cory

The loveliness of Paris
Seems somehow sadly gay.
The glory that was Rome
Is of another day.
I've been terribly alone
And forgotten in Manhattan
I'm going home
To my city by the bay.

I left my heart in San Francisco
High on the hill it calls to me.
To be where little cable cars
Climb halfway to the stars!
The morning fog may chill the air.
I don't care!

My love waits there in San Francisco
Above the blue and windy sea.
When I come home to you San Francisco
Your golden sun will shine for me!

I Know Where I'm Going

I know where I'm going and I know who's going with me
I know who I love but the dear knows who I'll marry.

Some will say he's dark, some will say he's bonny
But fairest of them all is my handsome noble Johnny

I have stockings of silk, shoes of fine green leather
Combs to bind my hair and a ring for every finger

Feather beds are soft and painted rooms are bonny
But I would leave them all to be with my darling Johnny

I know where I'm going and I know who's going with me
I know who I love but the dear knows who I'll marry.

Killing Me Softly With His Song

Fox/Gimbel

I heard he sang a good song
I heard he had a style
And so I came to see him
To listen for a while
And there he was this young boy
A stranger to my eyes

Refrain
Strumming my pain with his fingers
Singing my life with his words
Killing me softly with his song
Killing me softly with his song
Telling my whole life with his words
Killing me softly with his song

I felt all flushed with fever
Embarassed by the crowd
I felt he found my letters
And read each one out loud
I prayed that he would finish
But he just kept right on

Refrain Strumming my pain.....

He sang as if he knew me
In all my dark despair
And then he looked right through me
As if I wasn't there
But he was there this stranger
Singing clear and strong

Refrain Strumming my pain.....

Love is all Around

Reg Presley

I feel it in my fingers
I feel it in my toes.
Love is all around me
And so the feeling grows

It's written on the wind
It's everywhere I go
So if you really love me
Come and let it show.

Refrain
You know I love you, I always will
My mind's made up by the way that I feel.
There's no beginning there'll be no end
'Cause on my love you can depend.

I see your face before me
As I lay on my bed
I kinda get to thinking
Of all the things you said.

You gave your promise to me
And I gave mine to you
I need someone beside me
In everything I do

Refrain You know I love you......

Do You Know the Way to San Jose?

Hal David/Burt Bacharach

Do you know the way to San Jose?
I've been away so long
I may be wrong and lose my way
Do you know the way to San Jose?
I'm going back to find some piece of mind in
San Jose

L.A. is a great big freeway
Put a hundred down and buy a car
In a week maybe two, they'll make you a star
Weeks turn into years, how quickly they pass
And all the stars that never were
Are parking cars and pumping gas

You can really breathe in San Jose
They've got a lot of space
There'll be a place where I can stay
I was born and raised in San Jose
I'm going back to find some peace of mind in
San Jose

Fame and Fortune is a magnet
It can pull you far away from home
With a dream in your heart you're never alone
Dreams turn into dust and blow away
And there you are without a friend
You pack your car and ride away
I've got lots of friends in San Jose
Do you know the way to San Jose.......

I Could Have Danced All Night

Lerner/Loewe

Bed! Bed! I couldn't go to bed!
My head's too light to try to set it down!
Sleep! Sleep! I couldn't sleep tonight.
Not for all the jewels in the crown!

* I could have danced all night!
I could have danced all night!
And still have begged for more.
I could have spread my wings
And done a thousand things
I've never done before.
I'll never know what made it so exciting;
Why all at once my heart took flight.
I only know when he
Began to dance with
me
I could have
danced, danced,
Danced all night!

Repeat * I could
have danced.....

Will You Go, Lassie, Go?

Oh, the summertime is coming
And the trees are sweetly blooming
And the wild mountain thyme
Grows around the blooming heather,
Will ye go, lassie, go?

Refrain
And we'll all go together
To pluck wild mountain thyme,
All around the blooming heather,
Will ye go, lassie, go?

I will build my love a tower
Near yon pure crystal fountain,
And on it I will pile
All the flowers of the mountain,
Will ye go, lassie, go?

Refrain And we'll all.......

If my true love she were gone,
I would surely find another,
Where wild mountain thyme
Grows around the blooming heather,
Will ye go, lassie, go?

Refrain And we'll all.......

I've Got you Under My Skin

Cole Porter

I've got you under my skin
I've got you deep in the
heart of me
So deep in my heart,
That you're really a part
of me
I've got you under my skin

I've tried so not to give in
I've said to myself
This affair never will go so well
But why should I try to resist,
When baby I know damn well
That I've got you under my skin

I'd sacrifice anything come what might
For the sake of having you near
In spite of a warning voice
That comes in the night
And repeats, repeats in my ear

Don't you know you fool, you never can win
Use your mentality, wake up to reality
But each time I do, just the thought of you
Makes me stop before I begin
'Cause I've got you under my skin

Happy Together

Garry Bonner/Alan Gordon

Imagine me and you, I do
I think about you day and night, it's only right
To think about the girl you love and hold her tight
So happy together

If I should call you up, invest a dime
And you say you belong to me and ease my mind
Imagine how the world could be, so very fine
So happy together

I can see me lovin' nobody but you
For all my life
When you're with me, baby, the skies'll be blue
For all my life

Me and you and you and me
No matter how they toss the dice, it has to be
The only one for me is you, and you for me
So happy together, so happy together

The Jug Of Punch

One pleasant evening in the month of June
As I was sitting with my glass and spoon,
A small bird sat on an ivy bush
And the song he sang was The Jug of Punch.

Refrain
Toora-loora-la, Toora-loora-lay, Toora-loora-la,
Toora-loora-lay
A small bird sat on an ivy bush
And the song he sang was The Jug of Punch.

What more diversion can a man desire
Than to sit him down by a snug coal fire
And upon his knee have a pretty wench
And upon his table a jug of punch.

Refrain Toora-loora-la........

But when I'm dead and within my grave
No costly tombstone will I have
They'll dig a grave both wide and deep
With a jug of punch at my head and feet.

Refrain Toora-loora-la........

Can You Feel The Love Tonight

Elton John/Tim Rice

There's a calm surrender
To the rush of day
When the heat of the rolling world
Can be turned away
An enchanted moment
And it sees me through
It's enough for this restless warrior
Just to be with you

Refrain
And can you feel the love tonight?
It is where we are
It's enough for this wide eyed wanderer
That we got this far
And can you feel the love tonight
How it's laid to rest
It's enough to make kings and vagabonds
Believe the very best

There's a time for ev'ryone
If they only learn
That the twisting kaleidoscope
Moves us all in turn
There's a rhyme and reason
To the wild outdoors
When the heart of this starcrossed voyager
Beats in time with yours

Refrain And can you feel ....

Crying

Roy Orbison/Joe Melson

I was all right for a while
I could smile for a while
But I saw you last night
You held my hand so tight
When you stopped to say hello
You wished me well
You couldn't tell that

I've been crying over you,
Crying over you and you said so long
Left me standing all alone,
Alone and crying, crying, crying, crying
It's hard to understand
But the touch of your hand
Can start me crying

I thought that I was over you
But it's true, so true
I love you even more than I did before
But darling, what can I do?
For you don't love me and I'll always be

Crying over you, crying over you
Yes now you're gone
And from this moment on,
I'll be crying, crying, crying, crying
Yeah, crying, crying over
you

My Favourite Things (modified)

There are rumours going around that Julie Andrews did a concert recently for retired people. Ms. Andrews sang a favourite from the Sound of Music. However, she changed the words to suit her audience:-

Eye drops and nose drops
And needles for knitting,
Walkers and handrails and new dental fittings,
Bundles of magazines tied up in string,
These are a few of my favourite things.

Crutches and cataracts
And hearing aids and glasses,
Polident and Fixodent and false teeth in glasses,
Pacemakers, golf carts and porches with swings,
These are a few of my favourite things.

When the pipes leak,
When the bones creak,
When the knees go bad,
I simply remember my favourite things,
And then I don't feel so bad.

Hot tea and crumpets,
And corn pads for bunions,
No spicy hot food or food cooked with onions,
Bathrobes and heat pads
And hot meals they bring,
These are a few of my favourite things.

Back pains, confused brains,
And no fear of sinnin',
Thin bones and fractures
And hair that is thinnin',
And we won't mention
Our short shrunken frames,
When we remember our favourite things.

When the joints ache,
When the hips break,
When the eyes grow dim,
Then I remember the great life I've had,
And then I don't feeeeeel, so baaaaaaad!

From A Distance

Julie Gold

From a distance the world looks blue and green,
And the snow-capped mountains white.
From a distance the ocean meets the stream
And the eagle takes to flight.
From a distance there is harmony
And it echoes through the land.
It's the voice of hope, it's the voice of peace,
It's the voice of every man.

Refrain
God is watching us, God is watching us,
God is watching us from a distance.

From a distance we all have enough
And no one is in need.
There are no guns, no bombs, no diseases,
No hungry mouths to feed.
From a distance we are instruments
Marching in a common band
Playing songs of hope, playing songs of peace,
They're the songs of every man.

Refrain God is watching us.........

From a distance you look like my friend
Even though we are at war.
From a distance I can't comprehend
What all this war is for.
From a distance there is harmony,
And it echoes through the land.
It's the voice of hopes, it's the love of loves.
It's the heart of every man.

It's the hope of hopes, it's the love of loves
It's the song of every man

Only You (And You Alone)

Buck Ram/Ande Rand

Only you can make this world seem right
Only you can make the darkness bright
Only you and you alone
Can thrill me like you do
And fill my heart with love
For only you

Only you can make this change in me
For it's true, you are my destiny
When you hold my hand
I understand the magic that you do
You're my dream come true
My one and only you

Love Is Teasing

Refrain
Oh love is teasing and love is pleasing,
And love is a pleasure when first it's new.
But as love grows older sure love grows colder
And fades away like the morning dew.

I left my father, I left my mother;
I left all my sisters and brothers too
I left all my friends and my own relations;
I left them all for to follow you.

Refrain Oh love is teasing........

And love and porter make a young man older;
And lovc and whiskey make an old man grey
What cannot be cured, love, must be endured, love;
And now I am bound for Americay.

Refrain Oh love is teasing........

I wish, I wish, I wish in vain
I wish that I was a maid again
But a maid again I can never be
Till apples grow on an ivy tree.

Refrain Oh love is teasing........

Oh, Pretty Woman

Roy Orbison/Bill Dees

Pretty woman, walkin' down the street,
Pretty woman the kind I like to meet,
Pretty woman I don't believe you,
You're not the truth
No one could look as good as you, mercy!

Pretty woman, won't you pardon me?
Pretty woman, I couldn't help but see,
Pretty woman, that you look lovely as can be.
Are you lonely just like me? wow!

Pretty woman, stop awhile.
Pretty woman, talk awhile
Pretty woman, give your smile to me.
Pretty woman, yeah, yeah, yeah
Pretty woman, look my way
Pretty woman, say you'll stay with me

'Cause I need you, I'll treat you right
Come with me baby, be mine tonight

Pretty woman, don't walk on by
Pretty woman, don't make me cry
Pretty woman, don't walk away, hey, o.k.
If that's the way it must be, o.k.
I guess I'll go on home, it's late.
There'll be tomorrow night, but wait!
What do I see? Is she walking back to me?
Yeah, she's walking back to me,
Oh, oh, pretty woman

Mamma Mia

Andersson/Ulvaeus

I've been cheated by you since I don't know when
So I made up my mind, it must come to an end
Look at me now, will I ever learn?
I don't know how, but I suddenly lose control
There's a fire within my soul
Just one look and I can hear a bell ring
One more look and I forget everything, oooh

Refrain
Mamma Mia, here I go again
My, my, how can I resist you
Mamma Mia, does it show again
My, my, just how much I've missed you
Yes, I've been broken hearted
Blue since the day we parted
Why, why, did I ever let you go
Mamma Mia, now I really know
My, my, I could never let you go.

I've been angry and sad about things that you do
I can't count all the times that
I've told you we're through
And when you go, when you slam the door
I think you know that you won't be away too long
You know that I'm not that strong
Just one look and I can hear a bell ring
One more look and I forget everything, oooh

Mamma Mia, here I go again
My, my, how can I resist you
Mamma Mia, does it show again
My, my, just how much I missed you
Yes, I've been broken hearted
Blue since the day we parted
Why, why, did I ever let you go
Mamma Mia, even if I say
Bye bye, leave me now or never
Mamma Mia, it's a game we play
Bye bye, doesn't mean forever

Refrain Mamma Mia.....

Gortnamona

Long, long ago in the woods of Gortnamona,
I thought the birds were singing in the blackthorn tree;
But oh! it was my heart that was ringing, ringing, ringing,
With the joy that you were bringing, O my love, to me

Long, long ago, in the woods of Gortnamona,
I thought the wind was sighing round the blackthorn tree;
But oh! it was the banshee that was crying, crying, crying,
And I knew my love was dying far across the sea

Now if you go through the woods of Gortnamona
You hear the raindrops creeping through the blackthorn tree.
But oh! it is the tears I am weeping, weeping, weeping,
For the loved one that is sleeping far away from me

24 Hours From Tulsa

Bacharach/David

Dearest, Darlin' I had to write
To say that I won't be home anymore
'Cos somethin' happened to me
While I was driving home
And I'm not the same anymore

Oh I was only 24 hours from Tulsa
Ah only one day away from your arms
I saw a welcoming light and
Stopped to rest for the night
And that is when I saw her as I pulled in
Outside of a small motel
She was there and so I walked up to her
Asked where I could get something to eat
And she showed me where

Oh I was only 24 hours from Tulsa
Ah only one day away from your arms
She took me to a cafe, I asked her
If she would stay, she said 'okay'

Oh I was only 24 hours from Tulsa
Ah only one day away from your arms
Oh the jukebox started to play
And night-time turned into day
As we were dancing closely
All of a sudden I lost control as
I held her charms
And I caressed her, kissed her, told her
I'd die before I let her out of my arms

Oh I was only 24 hours from Tulsa
Ah only one day away from your arms

I hate to do this to you
But I love somebody new
What can I do
And I can never never never go home again

The Nightingale

As I went a-a walking one morning in May.
I met a young couple who fondly did stray.
One was a pretty maid so sweet and so fair.
And the other one was a soldier and a brave grenadier.

Refrain
And they kissed so sweet and comforting as they clung to each other
They went arm in arm along the road like sister and brother
They went arm in arm along the road till they came to a stream
And they both sat down together for to hear the nightingale sing.

Oh soldier, handsome soldier will you marry me
Oh no said the soldier that never can be
For I have a wife at home in my own country
And she is the sweetest little flower that you ever did see.
Refrain And they kissed.......

Now I am off to India for seven long years
Drinking wine and strong whiskey instead of cold beers
And if ever I return again it will be in the spring
And we'll both sit down together for to hear the nightingale sing.
Refrain And they kissed.....

Old Maid in the Garret

I was told by my aunt, I was told by my mother
That going to a wedding would soon bring on another
Then, if that be so, sure I'd go without a bidding,
Oh, kind providence, won't you send me to a wedding.

Refrain
And it's Oh dear me, how will it be,
If I die an old maid in the garret?

Now there's my sister Jean, she's not handsome or good-looking
Scarcely sixteen and a feller she was courtin'
Now she's twenty-four with a son and a daughter,
Here I am forty-five and I never had an offer.

Refrain (And it's Oh dear me....)

I can cook, I can sew, I can keep the house quite tidy,
Rise up in the morning and get the breakfast ready.
There's nothing in this whole world that makes my heart so cheery
As a wee fat man, who'd call me 'his own deary'.

Refrain (And it's Oh dear me...)

So come landsman, come townsman, come tinker and come tailor
Come fiddler, come dancer, come ploughman and come sailor,
Come rich man, come poor man, come fool man, come witty,
Come any man at all that will marry out of pity.

Refrain (And it's Oh dear me....)

There's Always Something There to Remind Me

Burt Bacharach

I walk along the city streets you used to walk along with me,
And every step I take recalls how much in love we used to be.

Refrain
Oh, how can I forget you?
When there is always something there to remind me
Always something there to remind me

I was born to love you, and I will never be free
You'll always be a part of me, whoa oh whoa
When shadows fall, I pass a small cafe
Where we would dance at night
And I can't help recalling how
It felt to kiss and hold you tight

Refrain Oh, how can I forget you?......

I was born to love you, and I will never be free
You'll always be a part of me, whoa oh whoa, whoa oh whoa
If you should find you miss the sweet and tender love we used to share
Just come back to the places where we used to go, and I'll be there

Refrain Oh, how can I forget you?.....

Don't Let The Sun Go Down On Me

Elton John and Bernie Taupin

I can't light no more of your darkness
All my pictures seem to fade to black and white
I'm growing tired and time stands still before me
Frozen here on the ladder of my life

Too late to save myself from falling
I took a chance and changed your way of life
But you misread my meaning when I met you
Closed the door and left me blinded by the light

Refrain
Don't let the sun go down on me
Although I search myself,
It's always someone else I see
I'd just allow a fragment of your life
To wander free
But losing everything is like
The sun going down on me

I can't find, oh the right romantic line
But see me once and see the way I feel
Don't discard me
Just because you think I mean you harm
But these cuts I have
They need love to help them heal

Refrain Don't let the sun........

Anyone Who Had a Heart

Burt Bacharach

Anyone who ever loved could look at me
And know that I love you
Anyone who ever dreamed could look at me
And know I dream of you
Knowing I love you so
Anyone who had a heart
Would take me in his arms and love me too
You couldn't really have a heart and hurt me
Like you hurt me and be so untrue
What am I to do?

Every time you go away, I always say
This time it's goodbye, dear
Loving you the way I do
I take you back, without you I'd die dear
Knowing I love you so
Anyone who had a heart
Would take me in his arms and love me too
You couldn't really have a heart and hurt me
Like you hurt me and be so untrue
What am I to do?

(Hum melody of first four lines)
Knowing I love you so
Anyone who had a heart
Would take me in his arms and love me, too
You couldn't really have a heart and hurt me,
Like you hurt me and be so untrue
Anyone who had a heart would love me too
Anyone who had a heart
Would take me in his arms and love me too
Why won't you?

You Don't Have To Say You Love Me

Wickam/Bell/Donaggio/Pallavicini

When I said "I needed you"
You said you would always stay.
It wasn't me who changed, but you,
And now you've gone away.
Don't you see that now you've gone
And I'm left here on my own
Then I have to follow you
And beg you to come home.

Refrain
You don't have to say you love me
Just be close at hand
You don't have to stay forever
I will understand.
Believe me, believe me
I can't help but love you
But believe me
I'll never tie you down.

Left alone with just a memory,
Life seems dead and so unreal,
All that's left is loneliness
There is nothing left to feel.

Refrain You don't have to say.....

You don't have to say you love me
Just be close at hand
You don't have to stay forever
I will understand.
Believe me, believe me, believe me

Poems

We all love to hear a good poem recited well and with feeling. Here is a selection of poems; most are humorous, some sentimental, and a few more thoughtful.

Read through them all a few times and you will find some that appeal to you. These are the ones you choose. If you think of their meaning and feel the rhythm you will recite them well. Learn them off by heart, but if you think you might forget the words, bring this book and have it ready ......just in case!

London Streets

Christopher Matthew

Whenever I walk down a London street,
I take great care where I put my feet.
And I watch for the gobs
And the doggies' big jobs
That lie there in piles, some sloppy, some neat,
Waiting for people to squidge with their feet.
And I tiptoe around
With my eyes on the ground
And wonder what horror I'm next going to meet.

And the harder I look, I give you my word,
The more I seem drawn to the tiniest turd.
And the dogs see me coming and say, "Here's a sap.
Let's nip round the corner and have a good crap.
He's wearing those shoes that have crinkly soles,
With lots of small ridges and dozens of holes.
And if we distract him by having a piddle,
Nine times out of ten he'll tread slap in the middle."
There's nothing more pleases a dog's simple wit
Than to hear the familiar cry of 'Oh shit!'

On Being a Granny

Rosi O'Sullivan

I love being a granny, it's wonderful fun,
When up the path those little feet run,
And round your neck their arms entwine
With sloppy kisses and eyes that shine.
And it's "Come on Nana, come on, let's go!"
And it's hide-and-seek and peek-a-boo.
And on the swing and down the slide
And on all fours and piggy-back ride.
And soon poor Nana can play no more
So she gently collapses to the floor.

At last it's time for bed-time story
You snuggle together all warm and cosy,
When sleepy heads on pillows lay
This is the high point of the day.
They look like angels when fast asleep
You love them so, you want to weep.
Now off you go, get an early night
'Cause they'll be up before it's light
And trampoline upon your bed
And shout "Get up, you sleepy head."

So it's constant fun throughout the day
Until parents come and whisk them away.
Now is the time for gin and tonic
You've had your fill of fun and frolic!
And 'though you miss them when they've gone
They'll soon be back, it won't be long!

The Curlers Poem

Pam Ayres

A set of heated rollers
Is every maid's delight.
It stops you wearing curlers
In the middle of the night.
It keeps you looking spick and span,
When all the rest are not,
And though your hands are freezing cold,
Your head is nice and hot.

The Shawlie

Vincent Caprani

You can see her beyond in the snug
Wrapped in the ould black shawl,
Whisperin' softly to herself
And mindin' no-one at all.

She'll sip at her glass of porter
Prolongin' the dark delight
And tastin' the stored up mem'ries
That must last her through the night.

So let's buy her a bottle of Guinness
Or a glass of the warmer stuff
A drop of the 'how's-your-father'
To go with her pinch of snuff.

Golf After Many Y

Edgar A. Guest

For nine and twenty years they've said:
"Be sure you do not lift your head,
Then let your club-head follow through!"
Still something else I try to do.

For nine and twenty years I've known
The club-head must be outward thrown
To drive a golf ball straight and true.
Still something else I try to do.

For nine and twenty years the pro
Has told me what I surely know.
In his advice there's nothing new,
Still something else I try to do.

For nine and twenty years, the swing
I've known is just a simple thing.
Compact, precise, and timely, too;
Still something else I try to do.

And Billy Phelps, who plays with me,
Agrees that very shortly we
Shall celebrate, beside some cup,
Our thirty years of looking up!

The Ballad of William Bloat

Raymond Calvert

In a mean abode, on the Shankill Road,
Lived a man called William Bloat,
He had a wife, the curse of his life,
Who continually got his goat.
So, one day at dawn, with her nightdress on,
He cut her bloody throat.

With a razor-gash, he settled her hash,
O never was crime so quick;
But the steady drip, on the pillow-slip,
Of her life-blood made him sick,
And the pool of gore on the bedroom floor,
Grew clotted, cold and thick.

And yet he was glad that he'd done what he had,
When she lay there stiff and still;
But a sudden awe of the angry law
Struck his soul with an icy chill.
So to finish the fun so well begun
He resolved himself to kill.

Then he took the sheet off his wife's cold feet,
And he twisted it into a rope,
And he hanged himself from the pantry shelf -
'Twas an easy end, let's hope -
In the face of death, with his latest breath,
He solemnly cursed the Pope.

But the strangest turn to the whole concern
Is only just beginnin'!
He went to hell, but his wife got well,
And she's still alive and sinnin',
For the razor blade was German made,
But the sheet was Irish linen!

Don't Quit

When things go wrong as they sometimes will,
When the road you're trudging seems all uphill,
When the funds are low, and the debts are high
And you want to smile but you heave a sigh;
When care is pressing you down a bit
Rest, if you want, but don't you quit.

Sisters

Seamus Lavery

There was a young lassie lived over the hill,
She never got wed and it seemed never will;
And her fate was the topic all over the place,
Because she'd been born with a very plain face.

She had a young sister, a beauty so rare
That women and menfolk would just stand and stare,
And wonder why nature could be such a twister,
To give such a beauty, a plain ugly sister.

And even at dances boys deemed it their duty,
To dance all night long with this fair raving beauty,
Whilst there in the corner, left all on her own
Sat the poor ugly sister, forlorn and alone.

But fate has a strange way of turning things round,
And the poor ugly sister, a husband she found.
And the things people said then were really unkind
For the husband, though handsome, was totally
blind.

And when people spoke of his wife's ugly features,
He'd smile and he'd pity those talkative creatures,
Because visible beauty with age must depart,
While true love and beauty live deep in the heart.

There's an old wrinkled woman lives over the hill,
She never got wed and it seems never will,
For the youth and the beauty that once was her own,
She squandered and wasted, and now lives alone.

Caring Society

Christopher Matthew

Whenever I ring up, I get this reply:
'Customer Services
How may I help you?'
And when I have told them, they cheerfully cry:
'Bear with me, would you?
I'll just put you through.'

It could be the gas board, it could be BT,
It could be the council concerning our tree,
It could be the dealer about the new car,
Or a medical query that's rather bizarre
'Bear with me, I'm putting you through.'

It's always the same when they put you on hold:
'Our lines are all busy,
You're held in a queue.'
And, lest there be doubt, it's repeated tenfold:
'Our lines are *still* busy,
You're *still* in a queue.'

And so I just sit and I fume and I fret.
Is it worth hanging up? It's a pretty fair bet
That someone will answer me, just as I do.
And next time I'll go to the back of the queue
And once again hear that familiar coo:
'Hallo...
How may I help you?'

If

Christopher Matthew

I often wish that I were rich,
Then life would go without a hitch.

If only I were that Bill Gates,
I'd talk with kings and be their mates.

If I were Cameron Mackintosh,
My plays would make huge piles of dosh.

Just think, if I were Melvyn Bragg,
My face would be in every mag.

If I were Mr Richard Branson,
Without the beard, I'd be quite handsome.

I bet if I were John Paul Getty,
I'd dish out money like confetti.

If I were Sultan of Brunei,
I'd sell my place and buy Versailles.

The trouble is, there's just one hitch:
I'm poor as hell, and life's a bitch.

The Unisex Salon

Pam Ayres

O hand me down the aspirin, the warm sustaining tea,
Hold my feeble shaking hand and try to comfort me,
I went to have my hair done, I shall never go again,
They've made the salon unisex. They've started doing MEN!
A MAN was at the basin, leaning confidently back,
Though I hope like me it made his neck feel fit to crack,
I had to step across him, I can see his trainers yet,
And seeing him, I felt myself bedraggled plain and wet.

What's he doing here with us, breathing healthy spray,
Watching the assistants as they give the game away,
We come to be coloured, streaked and tenderly blow-dried,
And permed and titivated and WE WANT THAT MAN OUTSIDE!

Men should be in a barber's shop in a great big barber's chair,
Where a great big barber plies his trade in a great big pile of hair,
Where the carburettor's King, the wicket and the goal,
And men are in their rightful place beneath the barber's pole.

Why Joseph was accepted

Young Joseph Green was fain to wed
"Artistic" Minnie Brown,
But when he wooed she tossed her head
And wore an awful frown.

"No Sir," she said, "the man I wed
(I don't desire a saint)
Must have enough brains in his head
To learn to draw and paint."

Joe went away with heart quite faint;
I fear she'll ne'er be mine,
He sighed, "I cannot learn to paint,
'Twould take me all my time."

He sat him down once more to think
How he had best begin;
Oh, happy thought! "With pen and ink
I'll gratify her whim."

On wings of love he quickly flew,
And gained his Minnie's side;
"My darling! will this drawing do?"
"Oh,yes,"she quick replied.

Within his shelt'ring arms she flew,
Put hers around his neck
What think you, was it that he drew?
Not landscape, but - a cheque.

Wee Hughie

Elizabeth Shane

He's gone to school, Wee Hughie,
An' him not four,
Sure I saw the fright was in him
When he left the door.

But he took a hand o' Denny
An' a hand o' Dan,
Wi' Joe's owld coat upon him -
Och, the poor wee man!

He cut the quarest figure,
More stout nor thin;
An' trottin' right an' steady
Wi' his toes turned in.

I watched him to the corner
O' the big turf stack,
An' the more his feet went forrit,
Still his head turned back.

He was lookin', would I call him -
Och, me heart was woe -
Sure it's lost I am without him,
But he be to go.

I followed to the turnin'
When they passed it by,
God help him, he was cryin',
An', maybe, so was I.

Murphy and the Bricks

Dear Sir, I write this note to you to tell you of my plight,
For at the time of writing I am not a pretty sight.
Me body is all black and blue, me face a deathly grey,
And I write this note to say why Murphy's not at work today.

While working on the fourteenth floor some bricks I had to clear,
But to toss them from such a height was not a good idea.
The foreman wasn't very pleased, he is an awkward sod,
He said I'd have to cart them down the ladders in me hod.

Now shifting all those bricks by hand it was so very slow,
So I hoisted up the barrel and secured the rope below.
But in me haste to do the job I was too blind to see
That the barrel full of building bricks was heavier than me.

And so when I untied the rope the barrel fell like lead,
And clinging tightly to the rope I started up instead.
I shot up like a rocket till, to my dismay I found
That halfway up I met the bloody barrel coming down.

Now the barrel broke me shoulder as to the ground it sped,
And when I reached the top I banged the pulley with me head.
I clung on tightly, numb with shock, from this almighty blow,
And the barrel spilled out half the bricks some fourteen floors below.

Now when these bricks had fallen from the barrel to the floor,
I then outweighed the barrel and so started down once more.
Still clinging tightly to the rope me body racked with pain.
And halfway down I met the bloody barrel once again.

Now the force of this collision halfway down the office block,
Caused multiple abrasions and a nasty state of shock .
Still clinging tightly to the rope I fell towards the ground,
And I landed on the broken bricks that were all scattered round.

The barrel then being heavier it started down once more.
And it landed right across me as I lay there on the floor.
It broke three ribs and me left arm, and I can only say,
I hope you'll understand *why Murphy's not at work today.*

First They Came for the Jews

Pastor Niemöller

First they came for the Jews
and I did not speak out -
because I was not a Jew.
Then they came for the communists
and I did not speak out -
because I was not a communist
Then they came for the trade unionists
and I did not speak out -
because I was not a trade unionist
Then they came for me -
and there was no one left
to speak out for me.

Sister Agnes Writes to her Beloved Mother

Paul Durcan

Dear Mother, Thank you for the egg cosy;
Sister Alberta (from near Clonakilty)
Said it was the nicest, positively the nicest,
Egg cosy she had ever seen. Here
The big news is that Revd Mother is pregnant;
The whole convent is simply delighted
We don't know who the lucky father is
But we have a shrewd idea who it might be:
Do you remember that Retreat Director
I wrote to you about? - The lovely old Jesuit
With a rosy nose - We think it was he
So shy and retiring, just the type;
Fr P. J. Pegasus SJ.
Of course, it's all hush-hush,
Nobody is supposed to know anything
In case the Bishop - that young hyporcrite -
Might get to hear about it.
When her time comes Revd Mother officially
Will go away on retreat
And the cherub will be reared in another convent,
But, considering the general decline in vocations,
We are all pleased as pea-shooters
That God has blessed the Order of the Little Tree
With another new sapling, all of our own making,
And of Jesuit pedigree too.
Neverthless - not a word.
Myself, I am crocheting a cradle-shawl;
Hope you're doing your novenas. Love, Aggie.

GOD FATHER
EMMANUEL
CLAP FOR JESUS
DR. JESUS

Wheelie Bins

Rosi O'Sullivan

Our wheelie bins are black and green
They're big and ugly and shouldn't be seen!
They clutter up against the wall
Of houses neat and gardens small.
They stand like sentries on the road
Their smelly contents to off-load.
We pay by weight and pay by lift
And through our rubbish now must sift,
Instead of binning all in haste
We now must learn to compost waste!
Recycling paper, cans and tin
We throw them in our good green bin
And sneak our bottles out at night
The "smashing" noise a dreadful fright
Crikes! Did I really drink all that?
I must be quite a boozy pratt!
I really must go on the dry
And the "green living" give a try!

MIGHT-HAVE-BEENS

Anne Duffy, the Rhyming Rabbit

Golf's a game of might-have-beens;
Of putts we almost made
To each of us, it always seems
We scored worse than we played.

The bunker's lip;
That downward slip
Played havoc with our score.
The ricochet
Sent the ball away
Need I tell you more?

The awkward lie;
The chip rolled by
Instead of stopping near the pin.
That unlucky bounce
Killed the last ounce
Of hope, that we could win.

Yes, golf's a game of might-have-beens
That yet might be, someday.
They add visions to our dreams
And console us when we play.

Aunty

Edgar A. Guest

I'm sorry for a feller if he hasn't any aunt,
To let him eat and do the things his mother says he can't.
An aunt to come a visitin' or one to go and see
Is just about the finest kind of lady there could be.
Of course she's not your mother, an' she hasn't got her ways,
But a part that's most important in a feller's life she plays.

She is kind an' she is gentle, an' sometimes she's full of fun,
An' she's very sympathetic when some dreadful thing you've done.
An' she likes to buy you candy, an' she's always gettin' toys
That you wish your Pa would get you, for she hasn't any boys.
But sometimes she's over-loving, an' your cheeks turn red with shame
When she smothers you with kisses, but you like her just the same.

One time my father took me to my aunty's, an' he said:
"You will stay here till I get you, an' be sure you go to bed
When your aunty says it's time to, an' be good an' mind her, too,
An' when you come home we'll try to have a big surprise for you."
I did as I was told to, an' when Pa came back for me
He said there was a baby at the house for me to see.

I've been visitin' at aunty's for a week or two, an' Pa
Has written that he's comin' soon to take me home to Ma.
He says they're gettin' lonely, an' I'm kind o' lonely, too,
'Cos an Aunt is not exactly what your mother is to you.
I am hungry now to see her, but I'm wondering to-day
If Pa's bought another baby in the time I've been away.

Perfect Shot

Anne Duffy, the Rhyming Rabbit

The perfect shot!
As likely as not
You haven't a clue
Just how you played it,
Amazed, it
Went up high;
You saw it fly
And land near the pin.
Slowly, it rolled in.

A smile creased your face.
What an ACE!

The Dreamer

In the busy world of action
Where the race is to the strong,
Dreamers do not win prizes,
But they somehow get along.
Doers gather in the bakehouse,
Take the pastry and the bun,
But in missing things substantial
Dreamers have a lot of fun.

With his feet encased in slippers,
Seated in his easy chair
And his pipe at hand the dreamer
Can defy the world of care
Business in the street may bustle,
Commerce in the mart may hum
But that doesn't jar the dreamer
Or affect his kingdom come.

He can dally in the valley
Where the idle lilies lurk;
He can wander in the forest
When he ought to be at work.
When he should be chasing shillings
He can saunter down the street,
Calm, unmoved and quite complacent,
If he gets enough to eat.

Dreaming doesn't bring him money
Nor put treasure in his sack,
But it helps along digestion,
And it doesn't hurt his back,
He can analyse the struggle,
He can see unmoved the strife,
And if there is cause for worry
Shift the burden to his wife.

Methuselah

Methuselah ate what he found on his plate,
And never, as people do now,
Did he note the amount of the calory count,
He ate it because it was chow.
He wasn't disturbed as at dinner he sat,
Devouring a roast or a pie,
To think it was lacking in granular fat
Or a couple of vitamins shy.
He cheerfully chewed each species of food,
Unmindful of trouble or fears
Lest his health might be hurt
By some fancy dessert;
And he lived over nine hundred years.

The Volunteer Organist

The preacher in the village church one Sunday morning said,
"Our organist is ill to-day, will someone play instead,"
An anxious look crept o'er the face of ev'ry person there,
As eagerly they wathced to see who'd fill the vacant chair.
A man then staggered down the aisle whose clothes were old and torn,
How strange a drunkard seemed to me, in church on Sunday morn;
But as he touched the organ keys without a single word,
The melody that followed was the sweetest ever heard.

The scene was one I'll ne'er forget as long as I may live,
And just to see it o'er again all earthly wealth I'd give.
The congregation all amazed, the preacher old and grey,
The organ and the organist who volunteered to play.

Each eye shed tears within that church, the strongest men grew pale,
The organist in melody, had told his own life's tale.
The sermon of the preacher was no lesson to compare,
With that of life's example who sat in the organ chair.
And when the service ended, not a soul had left a seat,
Except the poor old orgainist who started towards the street,
Along the aisle, and out the door, he slowly walked away,
The preacher rose, and softly said, "Good brethren, let us pray".

I'm Fine, How're You?

There's nothing the matter with me,
I'm just as healthy as can be,
I have arthritis in both knees,
And when I talk, I talk with a wheeze,
But I'm awfully well for the shape I'm in.

All my teeth have had to come out,
And my diet I hate to think about.
I'm overweight and I can't get thin,
But I'm awfully well for the shape I'm in.

And arch supports I need for my feet,
Or I wouldn't be able to go out in the street.
Sleep is denied me night after night,
But every morning I find I'm all right.
My memory's failing, my head's in a spin,
But I'm awfully well for the shape I'm in.

Old age is golden, I've heard it said,
But sometimes I wonder as I go to bed,
With my ears in a drawer, my teeth in a cup,
And my glasses on a shelf until I get up.
And when sleep dims my eyes, I say to myself,
Is there anything else I should lay on the shelf?

The reason I know my youth has been spent,
Is my get-up-and-go has got-up-and-went!
But really I don't mind when I think with a grin,
Of all the places my get-up has been.

I get up each morning and dust off my wits,
Pick up the paper and read the obits.
If my name is missing, I'm therefore not dead,
So I eat a good breakfast and jump back into bed.

The moral of this, as the tale unfolds,
Is that for you and me, who are growing old,
It is better to say "I'm fine" with a grin,
Than to let people know the shape we are in.

Wrinklies

Christopher Matthew

When Viv and I go to the shops
For milk and bread and cheese and chops,
We look at all the wrinklies there,
Who shuffle round the shelves and stare,

And tell ourselves when we are old
Our hands won't shake, we won't lose hold.
And when we're halfway home, we find
We've left the cheese and chops behind.

The Business of an Uncle

Edgar A. Guest

It's the business of an uncle, which I've frequently expressed,
To buy the toys and candies which the youngsters like the best,
And although the dads and mothers must at times some joys refuse,
An uncle's proper function is to give 'em what they choose.

It may be a mother's duty now and then to mutter, "No";
And a wise and proper father should not every sweet bestow,
But with nephews and with nieces every uncle worth his salt
Should disdain all such restrictions and be generous to a fault.

Now I know the uncle business, in these very prosperous times.
He should always, on his visits, take a pocketful of dimes,
And of course if there is something which the parents have denied,
It's an uncle's job to buy it just to keep them satisfied.

It's the duty of the parents to be strict and very stern,
And to teach those little rascals all the lessons they must learn,
But an uncle's job is different. He's another sort of man,
And the business of an uncle is to spoil 'em if he can.

The Elephant

H. Belloc

When people call this beast to mind
They marvel more and more
At such a LITTLE tail behind,
So LARGE a trunk before.

A Few New Teeth

Edgar A. Guest

The dentist tinkered day by day,
With wax and sticky gum;
He built a model out of clay
And shaped it with his thumb.
He made the man a lovely plate,
With three teeth in a row,
And bars of gold to keep them straight,
Then said: "They'll never show."

"Go forth," the dentist told the man,
"As proud as you can be.
Those teeth are perfect. No one can
Tell they were bought from me.
Why I, by whom the work was wrought,
The truth had never known.
Were you a stranger I'd have thought
Those teeth were all your own."

While going out he bumped a miss.
"Excuthe me pleathe," he said.
The lady smiled to hear him hiss -
His cheeks went flaming red.
He met a friend upon the street,
Who joined him for a walk
And said: "Let's go where we can eat,
And have a quiet talk."

"I'd rather walk," the man exclaimed
"Leth thtay upon the threet,
For with you I thould be athamed
Thum tholid food to eat."
"New teeth?" the friend remarked, and low
The troubled man said: "Yeth!
My dentith thwore you'd never know.
However did you guetth?"

Grandparents

Rosi O'Sullivan

Grandparents used to have white hair
And sit and rest in rocking chairs.
He'd smoke his pipe and she would sew
And seldom out the pair would go.

Well, gracious me, how things have changed!
Now visits must be pre-arranged.
They play their golf and go to races
And jet off to exotic places.

They don't 'do' naps, they haven't time,
They send Emails and work on-line.
Granny's blonde and wears short skirts
And Grandad sports pink polo shirts!

And if they've time they'll babysit
They love grand-kids, they keep them fit!
They drink Danone, spread Benecol
It helps reduce cholesterol.

Perhaps sometimes they're in a panic
Because their lives are somewhat manic!
Hardly surprising, you will agree
'Cause they're coming up to eighty-three!

"I'm My own Granpaw"

Many, many years ago, when I was 23,
Got married to a *widow* who was pretty as can be,
This widow had a grown-up *daughter* she had hair of red
My *father* fell in love with her and soon this pair was wed.

This made my *dad* my *son-in-law* which changed my very life
My *daughter* was my *mother* 'cause she was my *father's wife*
And to complicate the matter even though it brought us joy
I soon became the *father* of a bonny bouncing boy.

This baby boy grew up to be a *brother-in-law* to *Dad*
He became my *Uncle*, oh! it made me very sad
For tho' he was my *uncle* it also made him *brother*
To the widow's grown-up *daughter* who of course was my *step-mother*.

My father's *wife* then had a *son* who kept them on the run
He became my *grandchild* 'cause he was my *daughter's son*.
My *wife* is now my *mother's mother* which makes me so blue
Because 'tho she's my *wife*, she's my *grandma* too.

And since my *wife* is my *grandmother* I am her *grandchild*
Every time I think of it, it drives me almost wild.
And so I have become the strangest case you ever saw
As *husband* to my own *grandmother*, I'm my own *granpaw*!
Yes, I'm my own Granpaw!

Shall I Compare Thee to a Summer's Day?

William Shakespeare

Shall I compare thee to a summer's day?
Thou art more lovely and more temperate:
Rough winds do shake the darling buds of May,
And summer's lease hath all too short a date:
Sometime too hot the eye of heaven shines,
And often is his gold complexion dimmed;
And every fair from fair sometime declines,
By chance, or nature's changing course, untrimmed;
But thy eternal summer shall not fade,
Nor lose possession of that fair thou owest;
Nor shall Death brag thou wanderest in his shade,
When in eternal lines to time thou growest:
So long as men can breathe, or eyes can see,
So long lives this, and this gives life to thee.

Solitude

Ella Wheeler Wilcox

Laugh, and the world laughs with you,
Weep, and you weep alone;
For the sad old earth must borrow its mirth,
But has trouble enough of its own.
Sing and the hills will answer,
Sigh, it is lost on the air;
The echoes bound to a joyful sound
And shrink from voicing care.

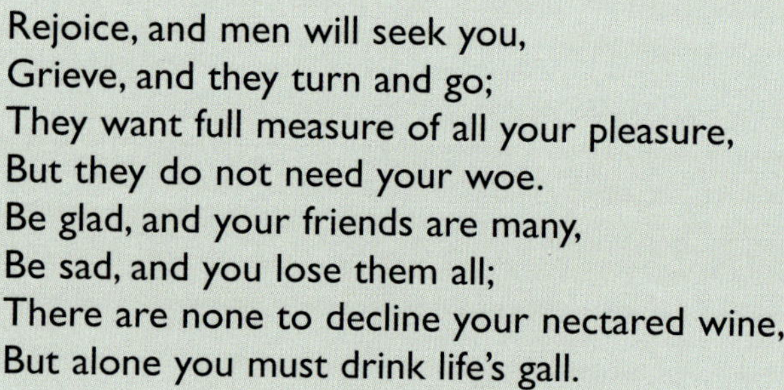

Rejoice, and men will seek you,
Grieve, and they turn and go;
They want full measure of all your pleasure,
But they do not need your woe.
Be glad, and your friends are many,
Be sad, and you lose them all;
There are none to decline your nectared wine,
But alone you must drink life's gall.

Feast, and your halls are crowded,
Fast, and the world goes by.
Succeed and give - and it helps you live,
But no man can help you die;
For there is room in the halls of pleasure
For a long and lordly train,
But one by one we must all file on
Through the narrow aisles of pain.

'All the world's a Stage'

William Shakespeare

All the world's a stage,
And all the men and women merely players:
They have their exits and their entrances;
And one man in his time plays many parts,
His acts being seven ages. At first the infant,
Mewling and puking in the nurse's arms.
And then the whining schoolboy, with his satchel,
And shining morning face, creeping like snail
Unwillingly to school. And then the lover,
Sighing like furnace, with a woeful ballad
Made to his mistress' eyebrow. Then a soldier,
Full of strange oaths, and bearded like the pard,
Jealous in honour, sudden and quick in quarrel,
Seeking the bubble reputation
Even in the cannon's mouth. And then the justice,
In fair round belly with good capon lin'd,
With eyes severe, and beard of formal cut
Full of wise saws and modern instances;
And so he plays his part. The sixth age shifts
Into the lean and slipper'd pantaloon,
With spectacles on nose and pouch on side,
His youthful hose well sav'd, a world too wide
For his shrunk shank; and his big manly voice,
Turning again toward childish treble, pipes
And whistles in his sound. Last scene of all,
That ends this strange eventful history,
Is second childishness and mere oblivion,
Sans teeth, sans eyes, sans taste, sans everything.

Sleeping Child

Edgar A. Guest

I like to tiptoe round her when she's lying fast asleep
And straighten out the covers where she's kicked them in a heap,
And when I find her sprawling kitty-corner on the bed
I find it fun to set aright that lovely sleepy-head.

Oh, whether late or early I'm retiring for the night,
I slip into her bedroom just to see that she's alright;
I stand and gaze upon her and I chuckle when I see
Her feet are on the pillow where her little head should be.

She's grown so very lively that she can't stay still at all.
The moment that she drops asleep she starts right in to crawl
And sometimes,like a woolly dog, as comfy as you please,
I've found her lost in dreamland with her head between her knees.

Oh, I have tasks that weary me, and tasks that I detest.
The mother's always calling me to work when I would rest,
But straightening out a little girl who's sleeping wrong-end to,
I'd call the happiest task on earth a father has to do.

Let Me Grow Lovely

Karle Wilson Baker

Let me grow lovely, growing old -
So many fine things do;
Laces, and ivory, and gold,
And silks need not be new;

And there is healing in old trees,
Old streets a glamour hold;
Why may not I, as well as these,
Grow lovely, growing old?

Rebbeca

Who Slammed Doors for Fun and Perished Miserably.

H. Belloc

A TRICK that everyone abhors
In Little Girls is slamming Doors.
A Wealthy Banker's Little Daughter
Who lived in Palace Green, Bayswater
(By name Rebbeca Offendort),
Was given to this Furious Sport.

She would deliberately go
And Slam the door like Billy-Ho!
To make her Uncle Jacob start.
She was not really bad at heart,
But only rather rude and wild:
She was an aggravating child....

It happened that a Marble Bust
Of Abraham was standing just
Above the Door this little Lamb
Had carefully prepared to Slam,
And Down it came! It knocked her flat!
It laid her out ! She looked like that.

Her funeral Sermon (which was long
And followed by a Sacred Song)
Mentioned her Virtues, it is true,
But dwelt upon her Vices too,
And showed the Dreadful End of One
Who goes and slams the door for Fun.

The children who were brought to hear
The awful Tale from far and near
Were much impressed, and inly swore
They never more would slam the Door.
- As often they had done before.

'How do I love thee? Let me count the ways'

Elizabeth Barrett Browning

How do I love thee? Let me count the ways.
I love thee to the depth and breadth and height
My soul can reach, when feeling out of sight
For the ends of being and ideal grace.
I love thee to the level of every day's
Most quiet need, by sun and candlelight.
I love thee freely, as men strive for right;
I love thee purely, as they turn from praise.
I love thee with the passion put to use
In my old griefs, and with my childhood's faith.
I love thee with a love I seemed to lose
With my lost saints - I love thee with the breath,
Smiles, tears, of all my life! - and, if God choose,
I shall but love thee better after death.

On Going Home For Christmas

Edgar A. Guest

He little knew the sorrow that was in his vacant chair;
He never guessed they'd miss him, or he'd surely
have been there;
He couldn't see his mother or the lump that filled
her throat,
Or the tears that started falling as she read his
hasty note;
And he couldn't see his father, sitting sorrowful
and dumb,
Or he never would have written that he thought
he couldn't come.

He little knew the gladness that his presence
would have made,
And the joy it would have given, or he never would
have stayed.
He didn't know how hungry had the little mother
grown
Once again to see her baby and to claim him for
her own.
He didn't guess the meaning of his visit Christmas
Day
Or he never would have written that he couldn't
get away.

He couldn't see the fading of the cheeks that once
were pink,
And the silver in the tresses; and he didn't
stop to think
How the years are passing swiftly, and
next Christmas it might be
There would be no home to visit and
no mother dear to see.
He didn't think about it - I'll not
say he didn't care.
He was heedless and forgetful or
he'd surely have been there.

Are you going home for
Christmas? Have you written
you'll be there ?
Going home to kiss the mother
and to show her that you care?
Going home to greet the father in
a way to make him glad?
If you're not I hope there'll never
come a time you'll wish you
had.
Just sit down and write a letter
- it will make their heart
strings hum
With a tune of perfect gladness - if you'll tell them
that you'll come.

The Song of Fionnuala

Thomas Moore

Silent, O Moyle! be the roar of thy water,
Break not, ye breezes, your chain of repose,
While, murmuring mournfully, Lir's lonely daughter
Tells to the night-star her tale of woes.
When shall the swan, her death-note singing,
Sleep, with wings in darkness furled?
When will heaven, its sweet bell ringing,
Call my spirit from this stormy world.

Sadly, O Moyle! to thy winter wave weeping,
Fate bids me languish long ages away!
Yet still in her darkness doth Erin lie sleeping,
Still doth the pure light its dawning delay!
When will that day-star, mildly springing,
Warm our isle with peace and love?
When will heaven,its sweet bell ringing,
Call my spirit to the fields above?

Come to the Edge

Appolinaire said
'Come to the edge'
'It is too high'
'Come to the edge'
'We might fall'
'Come to the edge'
And they came
And he pushed them
And they flew.

Muhammad Ali

(When refusing to join the Army to fight in Vietnam)

'I ain't got no quarrel with them Vietcong.'

Sea Fever

John Masefield

I must go down to the seas again, to the lonely sea and the sky,
And all I ask is a tall ship and a star to steer her by;
And the wheel's kick and the wind's song and the white sail's shaking,
And a grey mist on the sea's face, and a grey dawn breaking.

I must go down to the seas again, for the call of the running tide
Is a wild call and a clear call that may not be denied;
And all I ask is a windy day with the white clouds flying,
And the flung spray and the blown spume, and the sea-gulls crying.

I must go down to the seas again, to the vagrant gypsy life,
To the gull's way and the whale's way where the wind's like a whetted knife;
And all I ask is a merry yarn from a laughing fellow-rover,
And quiet sleep and a sweet dream when the long trick's over.

Amusing Stories

How often have you wanted to tell a joke but your mind was a total blank and the opportunity was lost? Here are some amusing stories and shorter jokes that you can prepare for the next occasion. Pick one that makes you laugh and memorise it well, but not word for word. It is better to tell it your own way. But always remember the punch line!

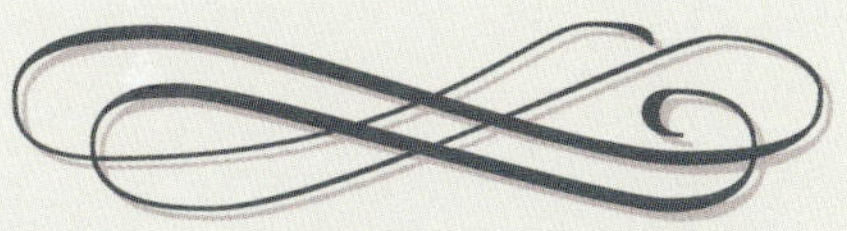

XV

Post Office worker

A Post Office worker at the sorting office finds an unstamped, poorly hand-written envelope addressed to God. He opens it and discovers it is from an elderly lady, distressed because some thief robbed her of 100 dollars. She will be cold and hungry for the rest of the month if she doesn't receive some divine intervention.

The worker organises a collection amongst the other postal workers who dig deep and come up with 96 dollars. They get it to her by special courier the same morning.

A week later, the same postal worker recognises the same hand on another envelope. He opens it and reads: "Dear God, thank you for the 100 dollars. This month would have been so bleak otherwise. *P.S. It was 4 dollars short but that was probably those thieving bastards at the Post Office.*"

Off to Rome

Mrs. Murphy said to her Parish Priest, "Father, I hear you are off to Rome. Would you say a prayer for me that I'll get pregnant at last and raise a family?" The priest said, "I'll do more than that, Mrs. Murphy. I'll light a candle in St. Peter's Basilica."

Eight years later he returned to the village and the first person he saw was Mrs. Murphy. She kissed his hand and said, "You're a living saint, Father. The three boys are at school, the twins are in the pram, and the two girls are playing in the yard."

He said "Glory be to God, and where's your husband?" She said, *"He's gone off to Rome to put out the candle!"*

A Religious Message of Hope and Inspiration

The Irish daughter had not been home in 5 years. Upon her return, her father cursed her, "Where have you been all this time, you hussy! Why didn't you write to us; not even a line to let us know how you were doing? Why didn't you call? You little tramp! Don't you know what you put your Mum through??!!"

The girl, crying, replied, "Sniff, sniff... Dad... I became a prostitute... "

"WHAT!!? Out of here, you shameless harlot! Sinner! You're a disgrace to this family - I don't ever want to see you again!"

"OK, Dad - as you wish. I just came back to give Mom this luxury fur coat, title deeds to a ten room mansion, plus a savings account certificate for 200 million. For my little brother, this gold Rolex, and for you, Daddy, the spanking new Mercedes limited edition convertible that's parked outside, plus a lifetime membership to the Country Club... (takes a breath)... an invitation for you all to spend New Year's Eve on board my new yacht in the South of France, and.... "

"Now, what was it you said you had become?"

Girl, crying again, "Sniff, sniff...A prostitute, Dad... Sniff, sniff. "

"Oh, bejesus - you scared me half to death, girl! I thought you said a **Protestant**. *Come here and give your old man a hug!"*

Speeding

A man and his wife are driving down the road when a cop pulls them over. The cop says to the man, "Do you know that you were speeding? The man replies, "No sir, I didn't know I was speeding." The man's wife then yells, "Yes you did, you knew you were speeding I've been telling you to slow down for miles." "SHUT UP!" the man says to his wife, "Shut the hell up, just sit back and be quiet."

Then the cop says, "well since I've got you pulled over, did you know that the tag on your tax disc is expired?" "No Sir" the man replies, "I did not know that." "WHATEVER!" His wife yells, "I've been telling you to go get it up-to-date for 2 whole months now!" "Shut up" the man yells to his wife again! "Sit back and shut up, mind your own business!"

Curious, the cop walks over to the woman's side of the car and asks her, "Does he always talk to you this way?" "No" she replies, *"Only when he's drinking!"*

Shepherd

A man along a road in the countryside comes across a shepherd and a huge flock of sheep. He says to the shepherd, "I will bet you €100 against one of your sheep that I can tell you the exact number in this flock." The shepherd accepts the bet, and the man says "894." The shepherd is astonished, because that is exactly right. He says "OK, I'm a man of my word, take an animal." The man picks one up and begins to walk away.

"Wait," cries the shepherd, "Let me have a chance to get even. Double or nothing that I can guess your exact occupation."
The man says "Sure".
"You are an economist in the Central Bank", says the shepherd.
"Amazing!" responds the man, " You are exactly right! But tell me, how did you deduce that?"

"Well," says the shepherd, *"put down **my dog** and I will tell you."*

Doctor, Doctor

A man walked into the office of the eminent psychiatrist Dr. Von Bernuth, and sat down to explain his problem.

"Doctor, doctor!" he started.

"No need to repeat yourself, my good man," replied the doctor. "One doctor is enough."

"Yes, well, you see, I've got this problem," the man continued. "I keep hallucinating that I'm a dog; a large, white, hairy Pyrenees mountain dog. It's crazy, I don't know what to do!"

"A common canine complex," said the doctor soothingly. "Come over here and lie down on the couch."

"Oh no, Doctor. *I'm not allowed up on the furniture."*

Millionaire

Once there was a millionaire, who collected live alligators. He kept them in the pool at the back of his mansion. The millionaire also had a beautiful daughter who was single.

One day, the millionaire decides to throw a huge party, and during the party he announces, "My dear guests, I have a proposition for every man here. I will give one million dollars, or my daughter, to the man who can swim across this pool full of alligators and emerge unharmed!" As soon as he finished his last word there was the sound of a large splash in the pool. The guy in the pool was swimming with all his might, and the crowd began to cheer him on. Finally, he made it to the other side of the pool, unharmed.

The millionaire was impressed. He said, "That was incredible! Fantastic! I didn't think it could be done! Well, I must keep my end of the bargain. Do you want my daughter or the one million dollars?" The guy catches his breath, then says, "Listen, I don't want your money! And I don't want your daughter! *I want the asshole who pushed me into the pool.*"

Teenagers!

The teenage girl was shopping for a dress and found one she decided to buy. "I love it!" she told the salesperson. "It's beautiful! I adore it!"

Then, as it was being wrapped, she grew thoughtful and asked the salesperson, "Just in case my mother likes it, *can I bring it back?*"

Cuts both ways

In a Shanghai bungalow shared by several young Europeans, the Chinese houseboy had a perfectly round head which he kept shaved and polished like a billiard ball.
The young men were always taking pot shots at this tempting target with paper pellets or giving it a pat as they passed by.
One day they decided it was a shame to keep annoying the boy, so they called him in and told him they had decided to stop doing it.

He replied: " Thank you, masters. I, very pleased. *Now I not make your coffee with* ***dishwater*** *any more.*"

Farmer

A farmer gets sent to jail, and his wife is trying to hold the farm together until her husband can get out. She's not, however, very good at farm work, so she writes a letter to him in jail: "Dear sweetheart, I want to plant the potatoes. When is the best time to do it?"

The farmer writes back: "Honey, don't go near that field. That's where all my guns are buried."

But, because he is in jail, all of the farmer's mail is censored. So when the sheriff and his deputies read this, they all run out to the farm and dig up the entire potato field looking for guns. After two full days of digging, they don't find one single weapon.

The farmer then writes to his wife: *"Honey, now is when you should plant the potatoes."*

Civil Servant

Three boys are in the schoolyard bragging of how great their fathers are.

The first one says: "Well, my father runs the fastest. He can fire an arrow, and start to run, I tell you, he gets there before the arrow".

The second one says: "Ha! You think that's fast! My father is a hunter. He can shoot his gun and be there before the bullet".

The third one listens to the other two and shakes his head. He then says: "You two know nothing about fast. *My father is a civil servant. He stops working at 4:30 and he is home by 3:45!!"*

Hobo

A hobo comes up to the front door of a neat looking farmhouse and raps gently on the door. When the farm owner answers, the hobo asks him, "Please, sir, could you give me something to eat? I haven't had a good meal in several days."

The owner says, "I have made a fortune in my lifetime by supplying goods for people. I've never given anything away for nothing. However, if you go around the back, you will see a gallon of paint and a clean paint brush. If you will paint my porch, I will give you a good meal."

So the hobo goes around back and a while later he again knocks on the door. The owners says, "Finished already? Good. Come on in. Sit down. The cook will bring your meal right in."

The hobo says, "Thank you very much, sir. But there's something that I think you should know. *It's not a Porsche you got there. It's a BMW.*"

Funeral

The widow takes a look at her dear departed husband just before the funeral and, to her horror, finds that he's in his brown suit. She'd specifically said to the undertaker that she wanted him buried in his blue suit; she'd brought it especially for the occasion, and she was distressed that the mortician had left him in the same brown one he'd been wearing when the lightning bolt hit him.

She demanded that the corpse be changed into the blue suit. The undertaker said, "But madam! It's only a minute or two until the funeral is scheduled to begin! We can't possibly take him out and get him changed in that amount of time."

The lady said, "Who's paying for this?" Seeing the logic to this argument, a very reluctant mortician wheeled the coffin out, but then wheeled it right back in a moment later. Miraculously, the corpse was in a blue suit.

After the ceremony, a well-satisfied widow complimented the undertaker on the smooth and speedy service. She especially wanted to know how he'd been able to get her husband into a blue suit so fast. The funeral director said, "Oh, it was easy. It happens that there was another body in the back and he was already dressed in a blue suit. All we had to do was *switch heads*!"

Dear Old Pals

A London taxi-driver, putting on a spurt to reach a railway station at a certain time, ran down a cart, upsetting the contents.
A policeman, confronting the taxi-driver, demanded his name.

"Michael O'Brien," came the reply.

"Indeed" said the policeman, "that's my name, too. Where do ye come from?"

"Cork".

"And so do I. Now just wait here a moment while I go over and *charge this man with backing into ye."*

The Flood

There was a big flood in Cork. This guy was standing in water up to his knees. Two men came by in a rowing boat and said, "Get in." He said, "Oh no, the Lord will take care of me."

A few minutes later he was up to his waist in water. Another rowing boat came by, and the guys in it said "Get in." He says, "Oh no, the Lord will take care of me."

Next, he was on a roof with the water up to his neck. A helicopter came by to help him. He said, "No, the Lord will take care of me."

Well, he drowned. He got up to Heaven and when he met the Lord he said, "What happened?" Thc Lord says "I don't know what happened - *I sent two rowing boats and a helicopter for you!"*

The New CIA Agents

Three men are going through CIA training, trying to become secret agents.
They finally got through all their written and physical tests when they are pulled aside by one of the instructors who took them to a small room with another room adjacent to it.

They brought the first guy's wife into the room and left her there. The instructor then loaded two rounds into a pistol, handed it to the first man saying, "Go kill your wife of *five* years." The trainee took the weapon, went into the next room. He came back out one minute later and said, "I can't do it." The instructor replied, "Then you fail, so get out."

The second candidate's wife was brought to the room. The instructor then loaded two rounds into a pistol, handed it to the second man and said, "Go kill your wife of *ten* years." The trainee took the weapon, went into the next room, but returned three minutes later and said, "I can't do it." The instructor replied,"Then you fail, get out."

Finally, the third candidate's wife was left in the adjacent room. The instructor loaded two rounds into a pistol, handed it to the third man and said, "Go kill your wife of *fifteen years*." The trainee took the weapon, went into the next room where there is silence for one minute. Suddenly, there was the sound of two gunshots, followed by a huge commotion in the room.

The third man came out finally, sweating profusely, and said, *"You gave me blanks, so I had to choke her."*

A Sample

A mean man received a letter from his aunt asking him to send his twin boys to her for a holiday as she had never seen them. She enclosed the money to cover their railway fares.

A few days later a boy presented himself at her house and handed her a note which read -

"Dear Aunt. Here is young Dan, one of the twins. *The other is exactly the same."*

Slow Golfers

A pastor, a doctor and an engineer were waiting one morning for a particularly slow group of golfers.
The engineer fumed, "What's with these guys? We must have been waiting for 15 minutes!"
The doctor chimed in, "I don't know, but I've never seen such ineptitude."
The pastor said, "Hey, here comes the greens-keeper. Let's have a word with him."
[dramatic pause]

"Hi George. Say, what's with that group ahead of us? They're rather slow, aren't they?"

The greens-keeper replied, "Oh, yes, that's a group of blind firefighters. They lost their sight saving our clubhouse from a fire last year, so we always let them play for free anytime."

The group was silent for a moment.
The pastor said, "That's so sad. I think I will say a special prayer for them tonight."
The doctor said, "Good idea. And I'm going to contact my ophthalmologist buddy and see if there's anything he can do for them."
The engineer said, *"Why can't these guys play at night?"*

The Wife's Cat

A man absolutely hated his wife's cat and decided to get rid of him one day by driving him *a mile* from his home and leaving him at the park.

As he was getting home, the cat was walking up the driveway. The next day he decided to drive the cat *five miles* away. He put the beast out and headed home. Driving back up his driveway, there was the cat!

He kept taking the cat further and further and the cat would always beat him home. At last he decided to drive *ten miles* away, turn right, then left, past the bridge, then right again and another right until he reached what he thought was a safe distance from his home and left the cat there.

Hours later the man calls home to his wife: "Jen, is the cat there?" "Yes," the wife answers, "why do you ask?" Frustrated, the man answered, *"Put that son of a bitch on the phone, I'm lost and need directions!"*

Another 40 years

A middle aged woman had a heart attack and was taken to the hospital. While on the operating table she had a near death experience. Seeing God she asked "Is my time up?" God answered, "No, you have another 40 years, 2 months and 8 days to live."

Upon recovery, the woman decided to stay in the hospital and have a facelift, liposuction, and a tummy tuck. She even had someone come to colour her hair. Since she had so much more time to live, she figured she might as well make the most of it.

After her last operation, she was released from the hospital. While crossing the street on her way home, she was hit by a car and died immediately.

Arriving in front of God she demanded, "I thought you said I had another 40 years, why didn't you pull me from out of the path of the car?"

God replied, *"I didn't recognise you."*

A Bad Shave

One Sunday, a minister appearing before his congregation with a bandage on his face, explained: "I was thinking about my sermon and cut my face." After delivering an unusually long sermon, the clergyman found this unsigned note in the collection box:
Next time, why not think about your face and cut the sermon.

The Ants and the Golf Ball

Once there was a golfer whose drive landed on an anthill. Rather than move the ball, he decided to hit it where it lay. He gave a mighty swing. Clouds of dirt and sand and ants exploded from the spot - everything but the golf ball. It sat in the same spot.

So he lined up and tried another shot. Clouds of dirt and sand and ants went flying again. The golf ball didn't even wiggle.

Two ants survived. One dazed ant said to the other, "Whoa! What are we going to do?"

Said the other ant: *"I don't know about you, but I'm going to get on the ball."*

CUTTY SARK

That's not my Job

This is the story about four people named Everybody, Somebody, Anybody and Nobody.

There was an important job to be done and Everybody was sure that Somebody would do it.

Anybody could have done it, but Nobody did it.

Somebody got angry about that, because it was Everybody's job.

Everybody thought Anybody could do it, but Nobody realised that Everybody wouldn't do it.

It ended up that Everybody blamed Somebody When Nobody did what Anybody could have done!

Flying to Spain

Two friends were flying to Spain for a short holiday. An hour into the trip, the stewardess came on the intercom and said, "The pilot has informed me that we've lost an engine. There's no need for alarm, though. We have three engines left and we'll just be an hour late."

About another hour into the flight she made a further announcement. "We've lost another engine. Don't worry. We still have two more, but we'll be another hour late."

One man turned to his friend and said, "Damn it. *If we lose the other two engines, we'll be up here all day."*

Seeing is Believing

Henry Ford once asked a young car engineer to name his chief ambition in life. The young man said it was to become very rich. Everything else was secondary.
Some time later Mr. Ford gave the employee a small package. When opened, it revealed a pair of metal-rimmed spectacles, but in place of the lenses was a pair of silver dollars.

"Put them on," Ford requested. And the young man did.

"Now, what do you see?" Ford asked.

"Nothing," the engineer replied, "the money blocks out everything."

"Maybe you should rethink that ambition of yours," said the famous car maker, and walked away.

yers

A ver/ successful lawyer parked his brand new Ferrari in front of the office, ready to show it off to his colleagues. As he got out, a truck came along, too close to the curb, and completely tore off the driver's door of the Ferrari.
The owner immediately grabbed his cell phone, dialled 999, and it wasn't more that 5 minutes before a policeman pulled up. Before the cop had a chance to ask any questions, the lawyer started screaming hysterically.
His Ferrari, which he had just picked up the day before, was completely ruined and would never be the same, no matter how the body shop tried to make it new again. After the lawyer finally wound down from his rant, the cop shook his head in disgust and disbelief.

"I can't believe how materialistic you lawyers are," he said. "You are so focused on your possessions that you neglect the most important things in life."

"How can you say such a thing?" asked the lawyer.

The cop replied, "My God, don't you even realise that your left arm is missing? It got ripped off when the truck hit you."

"My God!" screamed the lawyer.
"Where's my Rolex?!"

Travelling Together

A nun and a priest were going to a diocesan meeting and had to travel about 200 miles by car. On the way the car broke down and they had to look for somewhere to spend the night in a small town. There was one guest house and it only had one room vacant, so they had to share the room.

Well, they got themselves organised and the priest said, "I'll sleep on the sofa and you take the bed."

They got into bed and after a while the nun said "Father, I'm freezing." So he got up from the sofa and found another blanket and put it over her on the bed. A few minutes later she said "Father, I'm still very cold." So he got up again and put his coat over her.

After a while she said "Father, I'm still freezing and 1 don't think the good Lord would mind if we acted like husband and wife."

"OK," he said, *"get up and get another damn blanket yourself."*

A Safe Haven

A friend once complained to my sister about the difficulties involved in child rearing, especially the lack of peace and quiet rest.

"What you need is a playpen to separate the kids from yourself," my sister suggested.

So my sister's friend bought a playpen. A few days later, my sister called to ask how things were going.

"Superb! I can't believe it," she replied. "I get in the playpen with a good book and the kids don't bother me one bit!"

A Big Decision

In the hospital the relatives gathered in the waiting room, where their family member lay gravely ill. Finally, the doctor came in looking tired and somber.

"I'm afraid I'm the bearer of bad news," he said as he surveyed the worried faces. "The only hope left for your loved one at this time is a brain transplant. It's an experimental procedure, very risky, but it is the only hope. Insurance will cover the procedure, but you will have to pay for the brain yourselves."

The family members sat silently as they absorbed the news. After a great length of time, someone asked, "Well, how much does a brain cost?"

The doctor quickly responded, "€5,000 for a male brain, and €200 for a female brain."

The moment turned awkward. Men in the room tried not to smile, avoiding eye contact with the women, but some actually smirked.
A man, unable to control his curiosity, blurted out the question everyone wanted to ask, "Why is the male brain so much more expensive?"

The doctor smiled at the childish innocence and explained to the entire group, "It's just standard pricing procedure. We have to mark down the price of the female brains, *because they've actually been USED.*"

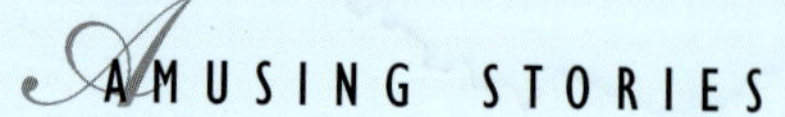

Friend or Enemy?

Once upon a time, there was a nonconforming sparrow who decided not to fly south for the winter. However, soon the weather turned so cold that he reluctantly started to fly south. In a short time ice began to form on his wings and he fell to earth in a barnyard almost frozen. A cow passed by and crapped on the little sparrow. The sparrow thought it was the end. But, the manure warmed him and defrosted his wings. Warm and happy, able to breathe, he started to sing. Just then a large cat came by and hearing the chirping investigated the sounds. The cat cleared away the manure, found the chirping bird and promptly ate him.

The moral of the story:

1. Everyone who craps on you is not necessarily your enemy.
2. Everyone who gets you out of the crap is not necessarily your friend.
3. And, if you're warm and happy in a pile of manure, keep your mouth shut.

Heaven or Hell

An engineer dies and reports to the pearly gates. St. Peter checks his dossier and says, "Ah, you're an engineer — you're in the wrong place."
So, the engineer reports to the gates of hell and is let in. Pretty soon, the engineer gets dissatisfied with the level of comfort in hell, and starts designing and building improvements. After a while, they've got air conditioning and flush toilets and escalators, and the engineer is a pretty popular guy.

One day, God calls Satan up on the telephone and says with a sneer, "So, how's it going down there in hell?" Satan replies, "Hey, things are going great. We've got air conditioning and flush toilets and escalators, and there's no telling what this engineer is going to come up with next." God replies, "What? You've got an engineer? That's a mistake — he should never have gotten down there; send him up here."

Satan says, "No way. I like having an engineer on the staff, and I'm keeping him." God says, "Send him back up here or I'll sue." Satan laughs uproariously and answers, *"Yeah, right. And just where are you going to get a lawyer?"*